PREVENTION OF ILLICIT TRAFFIC OF NDPS ACT 1988- SUPREME COURT'S LATEST CASE LAWS

CASE NOTES- FACTS- FINDINGS OF APEX COURT JUDGES & CITATIONS

JAYPRAKASH BANSILAL SOMANI

Dedicated

To

All the Past & Present Judges of the Supreme Court of India.

Salute to their wisdom.

Salute to their interpretation of Law.

Salute to their elaborative judgement writing.

SUPREME COURT OF INDIA

ppp

Contents

Contents

Preface

Dear Learned Advocates of Trial Court, High court and Supreme Court, Corporate and Individuals.

I am very delighted to provide you a book on PREVENTION OF ILLICIT TRAFFIC OF NDPS ACT 1988- SUPREME COURT'S LATEST CASE LAWS

In this book you will get...

1. Name of the Case i. e. Cause title

2. Relevant Sections discussed in the case

3. Hon'ble Judges/Coram of the case

4. Number of PDF Pages in Original Judgement of the case

5. All available Citations of the case

6. Case Note with appeal allowed/ dismissed or disposed off

7. Facts of the case

8. Hon'ble Apex Court's findings, while dismissing/allowing or disposing the appeal

9. Ratio Decidendi if any.

My special thanks to Manupatra, because of their web portal I can compile this book in well manner. I am also thankful to Notion Press to support me to publish & market this book throughout the Country. Thanks to my Juniors, Advocate Colleagues & Insolvency Professional Colleagues to support me in this venture.

Adv. Manoj Kumar Chowdhary & Adv. Shruti Kriti has helped me a lot to compile this book. I hope this book will add some value addition in the wealth of your legal knowledge. Your positive feedbacks will boost me to compile/ write further books & negative feedbacks will improve my skills. Kindly send your valuable feedbacks by email.

Thanks with Regards,

Jayprakash B. Somani

Advocate, Supreme Court of India

Email: jaysomani64@gmail.com

Web Site: www.jayprakashsomani.com

Call: 9322188701, 8459194576

ppp

Acknowledgements

Printed & Published by
Notion Press
No. 8, 3rd Cross Street,
CIT Colony, Mylapore,
Chennai, Tamil Nadu- 600004

ᐩᐩᐩ

Managed by
Jayprakash Somani Advocates & Solicitors
Law Firm for Supreme Court of India
Delhi Office
B- 851, 1st Floor, Shivaji Marg, New Ashok Nagar, Delhi 110096.
Call: 9322188701, 8459194576
Supreme Court Chamber
312, 3rd Floor, M. C. Setalvad Block, In front of 'D' Gate, Bhagwan Das
Road, Supreme Court of India, New Delhi 110001
Contact: 8459194576, 9811011747
www.jayprakashsomani.com

ᐩᐩᐩ

Download our app to get access to our Free Videos, Free Bare Acts, Free
Study Material in Legal as well as International Business Regime.
Android App Link ;-https://clpandrea.page.link/cmSm
Ios APp Link :-https://apps.apple.com/us/app/classplus/id1324522260
Login with org code ;- (qywzji)
Web Link ;-https://qywzji.courses.store/
Opportunity for Lawyers/ Social Workers to get Supreme Court Law
Firm JSAS's authorised centre at District Level.
Kindly Message or Call to: 9322188701

ᐩᐩᐩ

Books are available online in India
1. Notion Press:https://notionpress.com/author/jayprakash_somani
2. Amazon:https://www.amazon.in/s?k=jayprakash+somani
3. Flipkart:https://www.flipkart.com/search?q=Jayprakash%20Somani

Books are available online at International Market

4. Amazon International: https://www.amazon.com/s?k=jayprakash+somani

5. Amazon United Kingdom: https://www.amazon.co.uk/s?k=jayprakash+somani

6. E-Books/Kindle edition at National & International Level: https://www.amazon.in/s?k=jaypraksh+somani

❦❦❦

ONE

SUSHANTA KUMAR BANIK VS. STATE OF TRIPURA AND ORS. (30.09.2022 - SC) : MANU/SC/1262/2022

Relative Section:

Code of Criminal Procedure, 1973 (CrPC); Narcotic Drugs And Psychotropic Substances Act, 1985 - Section 19, Narcotic Drugs And Psychotropic Substances Act, 1985 - Section 21(B), Narcotic Drugs And Psychotropic Substances Act, 1985 - Section 22(b), Narcotic Drugs And Psychotropic Substances Act, 1985 - Section 22(C), Narcotic Drugs And Psychotropic Substances Act, 1985 - Section 24, Narcotic Drugs And Psychotropic Substances Act, 1985 - Section 27A, Narcotic Drugs And Psychotropic Substances Act, 1985 - Section 29, Narcotic Drugs And Psychotropic Substances Act, 1985 - Section 37, Narcotic Drugs And Psychotropic Substances Act, 1985 - Section 37(1); Prevention Of Illicit Traffic In Narcotic Drugs And Psychotropic Substances Act, 1988 - Section 3, Prevention Of Illicit Traffic In Narcotic Drugs And Psychotropic Substances Act, 1988 - Section 3(1)

Hon'ble Judges/Coram: U.U. Lalit, C.J.I., S. Ravindra Bhat and J.B. Pardiwala, JJ.

Equivalent   **Citation:**
2022(240)AIC236,AIR2022SC4715,2022(2)ALD(Crl.)929(SC),2023(122)ACC285, 2022 (3) ALT (Crl.) 251 (A.P.), 2023(2)BomCR(Cri)180, 134(2022)CLT928, 2022/INSC/1053, 2022 (4) J.L.J. R.318, 2022(4)PLJR357, 2023(1)RCR(Criminal)432

Number of Pages in the Original Judgment: 11

Case Reference:

Ashok Kumar v. Delhi Administration and Ors. MANU/SC/0052/1982; Sk. Nizamuddin v. State of West Bengal MANU/SC/0080/1974; Suresh Mahato v. The District Magistrate, Burdwan and Ors. MANU /SC / 0433/1974; Sk. Serajul v. State of West Bengal MANU/SC/0211/1974; Bhawarlal Ganeshmalji v. State of Tamil Nadu and Ors. MANU/SC/0394/1978; Shafiq Ahmad v. District Magistrate, Meerut and Ors. MANU /SC/0491/1989; Ashadevi v. K. Shivraj and Ors. MANU/SC/0057/1978

Case Note:

Narcotics - Detention - Legality - Section 37 of Narcotic Drugs and Psychotropic Substances Act, 1985 - Present appeal is at the instance of a detenu detained under Section 3(1) of the Prevention of Illicit Traffic in Narcotic Drugs and Psychotropic Substances Act, 1988 ('PIT NDPS Act') and is directed against the judgment and order passed by the High Court by which the High Court rejected the writ application filed by the Appellant herein questioning the legality and validity of the detention order passed by the Government of Tripura and thereby affirming the order of detention - Whether High Court rightly rejected the writ application thereby affirming the order of preventive detention?

Facts:

The order of preventive detention came to be passed essentially on the ground that in the past two First Information Reports (FIR) were registered against the Appellant herein for the offences punishable Under Sections 22(b)/22(C)/29 and 21(B) reply of the Narcotic Drugs and Psychotropic Substances Act, 1985 ('NDPS Act, 1985') and is a habitual offender. The first FIR is dated 05.11.2019 and the second FIR is dated 25.04.2021. At the end of the investigation of the FIR dated 05.11.2019, the charge sheet came to be filed and the trial is pending as on date. The investigation so far as the FIR dated 25.04.2021 is concerned, the same is shown to have been pending on the date of the proposal. However, what is important to note is that in both the aforesaid cases registered under the NDPS Act, 1985, the Appellant herein was ordered to be released on bail by the Special Court, Tripura. The Appellant questioned the legality and validity of the detention order by filing the Writ Petition in the High Court. The High Court vide the impugned judgment and order rejected the writ application thereby affirming the order of preventive detention. Appellant (detenu) is before this Court with the present appeal.

Held, while allowing the appeal

1. The requisite subjective satisfaction, the formation of which is a condition precedent to passing of a detention order will get vitiated if material or vital facts which would have bearing on the issue and weighed the satisfaction of the detaining authority one way or the other and influence his mind are either withheld or suppressed by the sponsoring authority or ignored and not considered by the detaining authority before issuing the detention order. [26]

2. In the case on hand at the time when the detaining authority passed the detention order, this vital fact, namely, that the Appellant detenu had been released on bail by the Special Court, Tripura despite the rigours of Section 37 of the NDPS Act, 1985, had not been brought to the notice and on the other hand, this fact was withheld and the detaining authority was given to understand that the trial of those criminal cases was pending. [27]

3. The preventive detention is a serious invasion of personal liberty and the normal methods open to a person charged with commission of any offence to disprove the charge or to prove his innocence at the trial are not available to the person preventively detained and, therefore, in prevention detention jurisprudence whatever little safeguards the Constitution and the enactments authorizing such detention provide assume utmost importance and must be strictly adhered to. [28]

4. The impugned judgment and order passed by the High Court is set aside. The order of preventive detention passed by the State of Tripura is quashed and set aside. The Appellant herein is ordered to be released forthwith from custody if not required in any other case. Appeal allowed. [29]

Disposition: In Favour of Accused.

ᴘᴘᴘ

TWO

RAJAN WORLIKAR AND ORS. VS. STATE OF KARNATAKA AND ORS. (04.05.2001 - SC) : MANU/SC/0280/2001

Relative Section:

Conservation Of Foreign Exchange And Prevention Of Smuggling Activities Act, 1974 - Section 3; Constitution Of India - Article 166(2), Constitution Of India - Article 22(5); Prevention Of Illicit Traffic In Narcotic Drugs And Psychotropic Substances Act, 1988 - Section 12, Prevention Of Illicit Traffic In Narcotic Drugs And Psychotropic Substances Act, 1988 - Section 3(1)

Hon'ble Judges/Coram: M.B. Shah and S.N. Variava, JJ.

Equivalent Citation: 2002(2)ACR1687(SC), AIR2001SC2303, 2001(1)ALD(Cri)877, 2001 (2) ALT (Cri)115, II(2001)CCR197(SC), 2001CriLJ2599, 2001(2)Crimes305(SC), 2001(75)ECC713, JT2001 (Suppl1) SC428, 2001(2)RCR(Criminal)756, 2001(4)SCALE16, (2001)5SCC295, [2001]3SCR512, 2001(2)UC240

Number of Pages in the Original Judgment: 5

Case Reference: Kamlesh Kumar Ishwar Das Patel v. Union of India MANU/SC/0732/1995

Case Note:

Prevention of Illicit Traffic in Narcotic Drugs and Psychotropic Substances Act, 1988 (P.I.T.N.D.P.S. Act) - Section 3 (1)--Preventive detention--Whether detention order bad in law for not informing detenu of his right to make representation to State Government?--Held, "no"--Information given about his right to make representation to detaining authority, i.e., Additional Chief Secretary to State Government--Order made by Additional Chief Secretary not as specially empowered officer but on behalf of State Government.

Undoubtedly, the order of detention shows that the Additional Chief Secretary and Principal Secretary to Government, Home and Transport Department is specially empowered under Section 3 (1) of the Prevention of Illicit Traffic in Narcotic Drugs and Psychotropic Substances Act, 1988. However, that by itself does not mean that the order of detention has been passed by him in his capacity as a specially empowered officer. If 'specially empowered officer' has exercised his power conferred upon him under Section 3 (1) of the P.I.T.N.D.P.S. Act, he would not have stated that it was by order and in the name of the Governor. The beginning of the order also would not be "Government of Karnataka", but it would be in his name. Further, the grounds of detention also make it clear, particularly para 28, that the order was passed by the Government of Karnataka. Therefore, it cannot be said that the appellants were not communicated that they were having right of making representation to the State Government. The grounds specifically provide that they have right to make representation to the detaining authority, the Central Government and P.I.T.N.D.P.S. Officers Board.

Facts:

1. These appeals are filed against the judgment and order dated 28th October 1997 passed by the High Court of Karnataka at Bangalore in Writ Petition Nos.42 to 48 of 1997 (HC). By the impugned judgment and order, the High Court rejected the contention raised by the appellants that the order of detention under the Prevention of Illicit Traffic in Narcotic Drugs & Psychotropic Substances Act, 1988 (hereinafter referred to as the PITNDPS Act') was illegal and void.

2. For the purpose of deciding these appeals we would refer to few facts pertaining to Criminal Appeal No. 763 of 1998. The order of detention was passed on 15th April, 1997 and has already expired on 23rd April, 1998. It has also been pointed out that trial against the appellant is pending for

the offences punishable under the NDPS Act. In the grounds of detention it is alleged the detenues had established factory where they were manufacturing Mandrax tablets which are psychotropic substances prohibited under the NDPS Act at the premises situated at Belgaum, State of Karnataka. A search was conducted in the aforesaid premises on 7th and 8th November, 1996. During the search it was found that premises had been converted into a factory where Mandrax Tablets were being manufactured by installing a tab letting machine, an oven and granulator etc. Appellant Rajan Worlikar was arrested on 8th November, 1996. He applied for releasing him on bail and was stayed by the High Court. Finally that revision application was allowed and the order releasing him on bail was set aside by order dated 17th April, 1998. During that time on 15th April, 1997, as stated above, order of detention was passed against him.

Held, while allowing the appeal

1. The learned counsel for the appellants next submitted that there is delay in making the order of detention and, therefore, the same is illegal and void. For this purpose, he submitted and appellant was arrested on 8.11.1996 and the detention order was passed after nearly 5 months i.e. on 15th April, 1997. In our view, this contention is rightly rejected by the High Court as the detaining authority has sufficiently explained the reasons for the said delay. The explanation given for the delay is also mentioned in para 4(C) of the counter affidavit filed on behalf of the Union of India. Considering the facts stated therein, in our view, the High Court has rightly rejected the said contention.[9]

2. No other contention is raised by the learned counsel for the appellants.[10]

3. In the result, these appeals a re dismissed.[11]

ᘒᘒᘒ

THREE

Pramod Singla vs. Union of India (UOI) and Ors. (10.04.2023 - SC) : MANU/SC/0349/2023

Relative Section:

Conservation Of Foreign Exchange And Prevention Of Smuggling Activities Act, 1974 - Section 3; Constitution of India - Article 19, Article 21, Article 22, Article 22(5);

Jammu And Kashmir Prevention Of Illicit Traffic In Narcotic Drugs And Psychotropic Substances Act, 1988 - Section 3; Maintenance of Internal Security Act, 1971; Narcotic Drugs and Psychotropic Substances Act, 1985; National Security Act, 1980; Prevention Of Illicit Traffic In Narcotic Drugs And Psychotropic Substances Act, 1988 - Section 3; Preventive Detention (Second Amendment) Act, 1952;

Preventive Detention Act, 1950 - Section 3, Section 3(1), Section 3(2), Section 7 to Section 9, Section 13

Hon'ble Judges/Coram: Krishna Murari and V. Ramasubramanian, JJ.

Equivalent Citation: 2023(245)AIC10, 2023 (2) ALT (Crl.) 11 (A.P.), 2023(2)BomCR(Cri)216, 2023/INSC/344, 2023(2)MLJ(Crl)475, 2023 (1) MWN (CR.) 481, [2023]2SCR793

Number of Pages in the Original Judgment: 17

Case Reference:

K.M. Abdulla Kunhi and B.L. Abdul Khader v. Union of India (UOI) and Ors. MANU/SC/0511/1991; Ankit Ashok Jalan v. Union of India (UOI) and Ors. MANU/SC/0276/2020; Pankaj Kumar Chakrabarty and Ors. v. The State of West Bengal MANU/SC/0052/1969; Jayanarayan Sukul v. State of West Bengal MANU/ SC/ 0040/1969; Sk. Abdul Karim and Ors. v. State of West Bengal MANU/SC/0059/1969; Frances Coralie Mullin v. W.C. Khambra and Ors. MANU/SC/0260/1980; Kamleshkumar Ishwardas Patel v. Union of India (UOI) and Ors. MANU/SC/0732/1995; Harikisan v. The State of Maharashtra and Ors. MANU/SC/0154/1962; Gian Chand v. Union of India and Anr. (Crl.) 39 of 2011

Case Note:

Criminal - Detention order - Quashing of - Acting on intelligence information, one consignment was examined by officers of Respondent No. 4 in airport and foreign origin gold was recovered from said consignment - Appellant being suspect, his shop was checked by DRI officials and gold was recovered from his premises - Respondent authority also conducted searches and arrested foreign nationals on grounds of finding incriminating evidence against them -Appellant along with other members of syndicate was arrested by officers of Respondent No. 4 authority, whereupon they were produced before CMM and sent to judicial custody - Appellant and other accused persons then sought for bail before CMM which was granted - Thereafter, DRIsent proposal to Respondent No. 2 to issue order of detention under COFEPOSA Act against Appellant, and subsequently Respondent No. 2 detaining authority passed impugned detention order as against Appellant - Representation was sent by Appellant to the Respondent No. 2 detaining authoritywhich was rejected - Appellant then filed writ in High Court seeking to quash detention order against him, which came to be dismissed - Hence, present appeal - Whether there exists incongruity between Pankaj Kumar case and Abdullah Kunhi Case and impugned detention order be quashed on grounds of sixty day delay in consideration of representation made by Appellant and illegible documents written in Chinese submitted to Appellant were grounds enough for quashing impugned detention order.

Facts:

An Intelligence was received by received by the Respondent that a syndicate of foreign nationals in association with some Indian Nationals were in the practice of smuggling gold into India through Air Cargo by concealing gold in transformers of electroplating/reworking machines etc.One such cargo was being imported to India and acting on the intelligence, the purported consignment was examined by the officers of Respondent No. 4 and foreign origin gold was recovered from the said consignment. The Appellant being a suspect, his shop was checked by DRI officials and gold was recovered from his premises.The Respondent authority also conducted searches at four different places and arrested foreign nationals on grounds of finding incriminating evidence against them. The Appellant along with other members of the syndicate was arrested by the officers of Respondent No. 4 authority, whereupon they were produced before the CMMand were subsequently remanded to judicial custody. The Appellant and other accused then sought for bail before the CMM, and he was granted bail. The DRI sent a proposal to Respondent No. 2 to issue an order of detention under the COFEPOSA Act against the Appellant, and subsequently Respondent No. 2 detaining authority passed the impugned detention order as against the Appellant. A reference was made to the Central Advisory Board, Delhi High Court, and subsequently, a representation was sent by the Appellant to the Respondent No. 2 detaining authority which came to be rejected. The Appellant then filed a writ in the High Court seeking to quash the detention order against him, which came to be dismissed.

Held, while allowing the appeal:

(i) In the COFEPOSA Act, since the detaining authority is separate from the Government, both, the Pankaj Kumar Judgment and the Abdullah Kunhi Judgment would apply, but in different spheres. The Pankaj Kumar Judgment, since it was rendered in the context of the Government being the detaining authority, would be applicable only to the detaining authority/ specially empowered officer under the COFEPOSA Act. The Abdullah Kunhi Judgment however, since it was rendered in the context of the COFEPOSA Act, the mandate thereunder would squarely apply only to the Government, and not the detaining authority. In simpler terms, this would mean that the mandate to not wait for the Advisory Board would be applicable only to the detaining authority. The Government, however, as per the Abdullah Kunhi Case, must wait for the decision of the Advisory Board. Since these two judgments exist symbiotically and apply to two separate authorities within the COFEPOSA Act, there exists no friction between the judgments, and hence there was no necessity for this point of law to be referred to a Larger Bench since the same was already settled.[34]

(ii) The Appellant-detenue, availing his rights sent a representation to both, the specially empowered officer and the Government. The detaining authority in the present case decided on the representation expeditiously and without waiting for the decision of the Advisory Board, and hence, did not violate the Pankaj Kumar Judgment. [36]

(iii) In cases of preventive detention, every procedural irregularity, keeping in mind the principles of the Constitution of India, must be accrued in favour of the detenue. In the present case at hand, the Appellant detenuehad been supplied with illegible documents in a foreign language. It was also important to note that these were the very same documents that the authorities had relied upon to detain the Appellant. [42]

(iv) Further, the principle of parity was squarely applicable in this case, since another co-detenue with identical circumstances, had already been granted the relief of quashing the detention order against him. In the case of Gian Chand v. Union of India and Anr, this Court while deciding on a quashing of a detention order, categorically held that in cases where a similarly placed co-detenue has already been granted the relief of a quashing of the detention order, the principle of parity must apply, and the same relief should be extended to other similarly placed detenues. [43]

Disposition: In Favour of Accused.

FOUR

Union of India (UOI) and Ors. vs. Saleena (29.01.2016 - SC) : MANU/SC/0117/2016

Relative Section:

Conservation of Foreign Exchange and Prevention of Smuggling Activities Act, 1974 - Section 3, Conservation of Foreign Exchange and Prevention of Smuggling Activities Act, 1974 - Section 3(1), Conservation of Foreign Exchange and Prevention of Smuggling Activities Act, 1974 - Section 3(3), Conservation of Foreign Exchange and Prevention of Smuggling Activities Act, 1974 - Section 8, Conservation of Foreign Exchange and Prevention of Smuggling Activities Act, 1974 - Section 8(1), Conservation of Foreign Exchange and Prevention of Smuggling Activities Act, 1974 - Section 11, Conservation of Foreign Exchange and Prevention of Smuggling Activities Act, 1974 - Section 13; Prevention of Illicit Traffic in Narcotic Drugs and Psychotropic Substances Act, 1988 - Section 3; Maintenance of Internal Security Act, 1971 [Repealed];Foreign Exchange Regulation Act, 1973 [Repealed] - Section 35; National Security Act, 1980 - Section 3(2); Jammu and Kashmir Public Safety Act, 1978 - Section 8; Jammu and Kashmir Prevention of Illicit Traffic in Narcotic Drugs and Psychotropic Substances Ordinance, 1988 - Section 3; Constitution of India - Article 19, Constitution of India - Article 22, Constitution of India - Article 22(5), Constitution of India - Article 32, Constitution of India - Article 226

Hon'ble Judges/Coram: Dipak Misra and Prafulla C. Pant, JJ.

Equivalent Citation: 2016(1)ACR1119, AIR2016SC641, 2016(2)AJR354, I(2016)CCR272(SC), 2016 Cri LJ1189, 2016(1)Crimes191(SC), 2 0 1 6 (1) EC r N 639, 2016/INSC/111, 2016(2)J.L.J.R.102, 2016(1)JCC470, 2016(2)MLJ(Crl)749, 2016(3)N.C.C.205, 2016(2)PLJR211, 2016(1)RCR(Criminal)905, 2016(1)SCALE682, (2016)3SCC437, 2016 (6) SCJ 478, [2016]1SCR373

Number of Pages in the Original Judgment: 20

Case Reference:

Devji Vallabhbhai Tandel v. The Administrator of Goa, Daman and Diu and Anr. MANU/SC/0133/1982 : AIR 1982 SC 1029; Lekha Nandakumar v. Government of India MANU/KE/0167/2004 : 2004 (2) KLT 1094; A.C. Razia v. Government of Kerala and Ors. MANU/SC/0034/2004 : AIR 2004 SC 2504; Saliyal Beevi and Ors. v. State of Kerala and Ors. MANU/KE/1870/2011 : 2011 (4) KHC 422; Babu v. State of Kerala MANU /KE/ 0882 /2009 : 2010 (1) KLT 230; Haradhan Sana v. State of West Bengal MANU/SC/0419/1974 : (1975) 3 SCC 198; Ashok Narain v. Union of India MANU/SC/0053/1982 : (1982) 2 SCC 437; Gurdev Singh v. Union of India MANU/SC/0706/2001 : (2002) 1 SCC 545; Ujagar Singh v. State of Punjab MANU/SC/0018/1951 : 1952 SCR 756; K.M. Abdulla Kunhi v. Union of India MANU/SC/0511/1991 : (1991) 1 SCC 476; Bhut Nath Mete v. State of West Bengal MANU/SC/0412/1974 : (1974) 1 SCC 645; Sunil Fulchand Shah v. Union of India MANU/SC/0109/2000 : (2000) 3 SCC 409; State of Tamil Nadu v. Kethiyan Perumal MANU/SC/0877/2004 : (2004) 8 SCC 780; State of Tamil Nadu v. Alagar MANU/SC/8213/2006 : (2006) 7 SCC 540; Chandrakant Baddi v. ADM and Police Commr MANU/SC/2465/ 2008 : (2008) 17 SCC 290; A. Sowkath Ali v. Union of India MANU/SC/0470/ 2000 : (2000) 7 SCC 148; Ahamed Nassar v. State of T.N. MANU/SC/0666/ 1999 : (1999) 8 SCC 473; Sanjay Kumar Aggarwal v. Union of India MANU/SC/ 0461/1990 : (1990) 3 SCC 309; Ashadevi v. K. Shivraj, Addl. Chief Secretary to the Govt. of Gujarat MANU/SC/0057/1978 : (1979) 1 SCC 222; Union of India v. Arvind Shergill MANU/SC/0572/2000 : (2000) 7 SCC 601; John Martin v. State of West Bengal MANU/SC/0136/1975 : (1975) 3 SCC 836; Khudiram Das v. The State of West Bengal and Ors. MANU/SC/0423/1974 : (1975) 2 SCC 81; Emperor v. Shibnath Bannerji MANU/FE/0010/1943 : AIR 1943 FC 75 : 45 CriLJ 341; Commissioner of Police v. Gordhandas Bhanji MANU/SC/0002/ 1951 : 1952 SCR 135 : AIR 1952 SC 16; Simms Motor Units Ltd. v. Minister of Labour and National Service (1946) 2 All ER 201; Machindar v. King MANU/ FE/0008/1950 : AIR 1950 FC 129 : Cri LJ 1480; Pratap Singh v. State of Punjab MANU/SC/0272/1963 : AIR 1964 SC 72; Raj Kishore Prasad v. State of Bihar and Ors. MANU/SC/0098/1982 : (1982) 3 SCC 10; Vijay Kumar v. State of Jammu and Kashmir and Ors. MANU/SC/0127/1982 : (1982) 2 SCC 43; State of Gujarat v. Adam Kasam Bhaya MANU/SC/0234/1981 : (1981) 4 SCC 216

Case Note:

Criminal - Detention - Order rejecting representation - Non-communication - Invalidation of detention order - Section 3(1) of Conservation of Foreign Exchange and Prevention of Smuggling Activities Act, 1974 and Article 22(5) of Constitution of India - High Court quashed detention order under section 3(1) of COFEPOSA Act, 1974 - Hence, present Appeal - Whether non-communication of order rejecting representation in effective manner would invalidate or vitiate order of detention

Facts:

Calling in question the defensibility of the judgment and order dated 24.10.2015 passed by the High Court of Kerala by which the Division Bench has quashed the order of detention passed against Abdu Rahiman (detenu), the husband of the Respondent, Under Section 3(1) of the Conservation of Foreign Exchange and Prevention of Smuggling Activities Act, 1974 (for brevity, 'the COFEPOSA Act'), the instant appeal, by special leave, has been preferred.

Held, while allowing the appeal

(1) While rejecting the representation, a speaking order need not be passed and what is necessary is that there should be real and proper consideration by the Government and the Advisory Board. The Constitution Bench has limited the application of principles of natural justice to the sphere of deliberation. It has confined it to real and proper consideration; application of mind. Dealing with the concept of fairness, it has been observed that fairness denotes abstention from abuse of discretion. Understanding the said principle correctly, it can be said that the use of discretion has to be based on fairness of approach. The authority concerned may not give reasons but there has to be application of mind.[18]

(2) Preventive detention is constitutionally permissible. The Courts can interfere where such detention has taken place in violation of constitutional or statutory safeguards. Treating the issue of communication of rejection of the representation by the competent authority or incorporation of the order passed by the competent authority in the order of communication as a constitutional safeguard, would not be correct. The duty of the Court in this regard is to see whether the representation submitted by the detenu has been rejected in a mechanical manner without application of mind. We are

inclined to hold that for the said purpose, the relevant file can be called for and perused.[23]

(3) On a scrutiny of the file, we find that the entire file relating to the detention was produced before the competent authority alongwith detailed comments. The said authority has clearly stated that he has gone through the representation and does not find any sufficient ground to exercise the jurisdiction under the COFEPOSA Act. In our considered opinion, this would tantamount to real and proper consideration, for the competent authority is not required to pass an adjudicatory order.[26]

(4) In view of the analysis, the decision in Lekha Nandakumar (supra) by the Division Bench of the High Court stating the principle that the order passed by the competent authority should be communicated failing which there will be a violation of the constitutional command engrafted Under Article 22(5) is not correct. The Court can always call for the file and peruse whether there has been rejection of the representation as required under the law.[30]

(5) The detaining authority on the basis of certain material passes an order of detention. The same has to be communicated at the earliest as mandated Under Article 22(5) of the Constitution. A period has been determined. Non-communication within the said period would be an impediment for sustaining the order of detention. Similarly, if a representation is made and not considered with promptitude and there is inordinate delay that would make the detention order unsustainable.[34]

(6) The Government has to follow the safeguards provided Under Article 22(5) and the provisions of the statute. It is because without a trial a person is deprived of his liberty. Promptitude of action within the statutory scheme is imperative. In the case at hand, these aspects which have been raised before the High Court have been negatived, and rightly so. On a scrutiny of the file which has been produced before us, we find that the competent authority of the appropriate government has passed an order on the basis of the material produced before it. It cannot be said that there is no subjective satisfaction. We may ingeminate that when the material, the file, the representation and the comments on the representation were produced before the authority and he had mentioned in the order that he had gone through the representation and not found sufficient ground for exercising the power Under Section 11 of the COFEPOSA Act, it cannot be said that there has been no subjective satisfaction.[36]

ÞÞÞ

FIVE

BIPINCHANDRA GAMANLAL CHOKSHI AND ORS. VS. STATE OF GUJARAT AND ORS. (10.12.2015 - SC) : MANU/SC/1456/2015

Relative Section:

Conservation of Foreign Exchange and Prevention of Smuggling Activities Act, 1974 - Section 3, Conservation of Foreign Exchange and Prevention of Smuggling Activities Act, 1974 - Section 3(1), Conservation of Foreign Exchange and Prevention of Smuggling Activities Act, 1974 - Section 3(3), Conservation of Foreign Exchange and Prevention of Smuggling Activities Act, 1974 - Section 6(1), Conservation of Foreign Exchange and Prevention of Smuggling Activities Act, 1974 - Section 8, Conservation of Foreign Exchange and Prevention of Smuggling Activities Act, 1974 - Section 8(2), Conservation of Foreign Exchange and Prevention of Smuggling Activities Act, 1974 - Section 9, Conservation of Foreign Exchange and Prevention of Smuggling Activities Act, 1974 - Section 9(1), Conservation of Foreign Exchange and Prevention of Smuggling Activities Act, 1974 - Section 9(2), Conservation of Foreign Exchange and Prevention of Smuggling

Activities Act, 1974 - Section 9(3), Conservation of Foreign Exchange and Prevention of Smuggling Activities Act, 1974 - Section 12A, Conservation of Foreign Exchange and Prevention of Smuggling Activities Act, 1974 - Section 12A(2), Conservation of Foreign Exchange and Prevention of Smuggling Activities Act, 1974 - Section 12A(3), Conservation of Foreign Exchange and Prevention of Smuggling Activities Act, 1974 - Section 12A(5), Conservation of Foreign Exchange and Prevention of Smuggling Activities Act, 1974 - Section 12A(6); Prevention of Illicit Traffic in Narcotic Drugs and Psychotropic Substances Act, 1988 - Section 3; Conservation of Foreign Exchange and Prevention of Smuggling Activities (Amendment) Act, 1975; Smugglers and Foreign Exchange Manipulators (Forfeiture of Property) Act, 1976 - Section 2, Smugglers and Foreign Exchange Manipulators (Forfeiture of Property) Act, 1976 - Section 2(2), Smugglers and Foreign Exchange Manipulators (Forfeiture of Property) Act, 1976 - Section 3(1), Smugglers and Foreign Exchange Manipulators (Forfeiture of Property) Act, 1976 - Section 5, Smugglers and Foreign Exchange Manipulators (Forfeiture of Property) Act, 1976 - Section 6, Smugglers and Foreign Exchange Manipulators (Forfeiture of Property) Act, 1976 - Section 6(1), Smugglers and Foreign Exchange Manipulators (Forfeiture of Property) Act, 1976 - Section 7; Maintenance of Internal Security Act; Jammu and Kashmir Prevention of Illicit Traffic in Narcotic Drugs and Psychotropic Substances Ordinance, 1988 - Section 3; Constitution of India - Article 14, Constitution of India - Article 19, Constitution of India - Article 21, Constitution of India - Article 22, Constitution of India - Article 22(5), Constitution of India - Article 352(1), Constitution of India - Article 352, Constitution of India - Article 358, Constitution of India - Article 358(1), Constitution of India - Article 359(1), Constitution of India - Article 359(1A)

Hon'ble Judges/Coram: J.S. Khehar and Rohinton Fali Nariman, JJ

Equivalent Citation: 2016(158)AIC23, AIR2016SC267, 2016 (92) ACC 906, 2016CriLJ650, 2016(1) Crimes126(SC), 2015/INSC/913, 2016(1)RCR(Criminal)418, 2016(1)SCALE50, (2015)16SCC59, 2016 (2) SCJ 233, [2015]11SCR1077

Number of Pages in the Original Judgment: 20

Case Reference:

Krishna Murari Aggarwala v. Union of India MANU/SC/0145/1975 : AIR 1975 SC 1877; Smt. Gangadevi v. Union of India and Ors.; Attorney General for India and Ors. v. Amratlal Prajivandas and Ors. MANU /SC /0774/1994 : (1994) 5 SCC 54 : JT 1994(3) SC 583; Makhan Singh v. State of Punjab; Union of

India v. Haji Mastan Mirza

Case Note:

Criminal - Legal propriety of detention order under COFEPOSA Act - Proclamation of emergency Under Article 352(1) - Constitution of India - Declared - State of Gujarat ordered detention of Appellant - Under Section 3(1) of COFEPOSA Act - Declaration under Section 12A of COFEPOSA Act issued - Detention of Appellant necessary for dealing with emergency effectively - On review Under Section 12A(2) - Competent Authority felt - Detention be continued - Emergency revoked by President of India - Same day - Order of detention against Appellant revoked - Appellant assailed order of detention - Filed Special Civil Application - Show Cause Notice issued to Appellant - Under Section 6 of SAFEMA Act - Meanwhile, one of brothers of Appellant - Approached High Court - Assailed a similar order of detention - Passed against him (brother) - Special Criminal Application filed - High Court held detention order violated Constitutional mandate - Article 22(5) - Set aside the order of detention of Appellant's brother - Two other brothers of Appellant - Likewise approached Court - High Court set aside their orders of conviction as well - Challenge raised by Appellant - Rejected by learned Single Judge - High Court relied on decision - Attorney General for India and Ors. v. Amratlal Prajivandas and Ors. - Appellant preferred LPA - Dismissed by Division Bench - Orders passed by learned Single Judge and Division Bench under assail - Whether in view of the judgment rendered by this Court in Attorney General for India and Ors. v. Amratlal Prajivandas and Ors., the right of the Appellant to assail the order of his detention stood foreclosed - Whether the Appellant had no occasion whatsoever to challenge to the order of his detention, on the grounds available to him, while the detention order subsisted under the limited scope of Section 3 of the COFEPOSA Act read with Section 12A - Whether the High Court's order of not allowing the Appellant to raise a challenge to the order of his detention is justified

Facts:

The State of Gujarat ordered the detention of the Appellant-Bipinchandra Gamanlal Chokshi, Under Section 3 (1) of the Conservation of Foreign Exchange and Prevention of Smuggling Activities Act, 1974 (COFEPOSA Act).

Proclamation of emergency Under Article 352(1) of the Constitution of India was declared on 25.06.1975. Based on the above, the State of Gujarat issued a declaration Under Section 12A of the COFEPOSA Act, that the detention of the Appellant was necessary for dealing effectively with the emergency contemplated Under Section 12(A)(2) of the COFEPOSA Act. Under Sub-section (2) of Section 12A of the COFEPOSA Act, every detention order has to be reviewed within fifteen days. It is in consonance with Sub-section (2) aforementioned, that the detention order passed against the Appellant was reviewed on 26.6.1976.

The Competent Authority arrived at the conclusion in the above review that the detention of the Appellant should continue. In compliance with Section 12A(3) of the COFEPOSA Act, the first review contemplated Under Sub-section (3) took place on 04.10.1976. Yet again, the order of detention of the Appellant was affirmed. Still further, the second review Under Section 12A(3) of the COFEPOSA Act, was held on 9.2.1977. Yet again, the Competent Authority arrived at the conclusion, that the detention of the Appellant should be continued.

Emergency declared Under Article 352 of the Constitution of India, was revoked by the President of India, on 21.3.1977. On the same day, as the revocation of the emergency, i.e., on 21.3.1977 itself, the State of Gujarat, revoked the order of detention passed against the Appellant.

The Appellant assailed the order of his detention by filing Special Civil Application. Thus, the challenge was made well after the order of his detention had been revoked. The grievance of the Appellant in assailing the order of his detention assumed significance, on account of a show cause notice issued to the Appellant on 28.4.1977, Under Section 6 of the Smugglers and Foreign Exchange Manipulators (Forfeiture of Property) Act, 1976 (SAFEMA Act). The initiation of proceedings under the SAFEMA Act against the Appellant, were based on Section 2 of SAFEMA Act.

One of the brothers of the Appellant, namely, Niranjan Dahyabhai Chokshi approached the High Court, so as to assail a similar order of detention, as was also passed against him. The challenge was raised through Special Criminal Application. The challenge to the detention of Niranjan Dahyabhai Chokshi was raised on the ground of the law declared by this Court in Krishna Murari Aggarwala v. Union of India. Having arrived at the finding, that the grounds of detention were not formulated at the time of passing of the order of detention, the High Court of Gujarat concluded, that the detention order, clearly violated the constitutional mandate contained in Article 22(5), and as such, set aside the order of detention of Niranjan Dahyabhai Chokshi (the Appellant's brother). Simultaneously with the setting aside of the above order, proceedings initiated against Niranjan

Dahyabhai Chokshi Under Section 6 of the SAFEMA Act were also set aside as unsustainable.

Two other brothers of the Appellant, had likewise approached the High Court of Gujarat by filing Special Criminal Applications to likewise assail the orders of their detention. Yet again, the High Court by its order set aside their orders of detention, based on the decision rendered by this Court in Krishna Murari Aggarwala v. Union of India.

Insofar as the challenge raised by the Appellant herein, to the order of his detention, as well as, the order of initiation of proceedings Under Section 6 of the SAFEMA Act on 28.4.1977 is concerned, the claim raised by the Appellant was rejected by a learned Single Judge of the High Court. The High Court relied on the decision rendered by a nine-Judge Bench of this Court, in Attorney General for India and Ors. v. Amratlal Prajivandas and Ors. Dissatisfied with the order passed by the learned Single Judge, the Appellant preferred an LPA. The said appeal came to be dismissed by a Division Bench of the High Court. The orders passed by the learned Single Judge in Special Civil Application and by the Division Bench in LPA have been impugned by the Appellant before this Court.

Held, while allowing the appeal

1. Having given its thoughtful consideration to the issue in hand, the Court was satisfied, that insofar as the factual position was concerned, the present case was apparently similar to the one adjudicated in Attorney General for India and Ors. v. Amratlal Prajivandas and Ors., on account of the apparent similarity herein within the factual position recorded. Thus viewed, the conclusions on the issue, should ordinarily follow the determination rendered by this Court in Attorney General for India's case.[16]

2. The Court's pointed attention was drawn to the factual position depicted in paragraph 41 of Attorney General for India and Ors. v. Amratlal Prajivandas and Ors., namely, that the detenu therein, had an opportunity to assail the impugned order of detention under COFEPOSA Act, and it is therefore, that this Court arrived at the conclusion, that a challenge having not been raised by the Respondent in the above case, it would not now be open to him to raise such a challenge, after the detention order stood revoked. Insofar as the present controversy is concerned, learned Counsel wishes this Court to believe, that there was no opportunity whatsoever for the Appellant to assail the impugned order of detention dated 11.6.1976.[18]

3. The Court finds merit in the contention of the earned Counsel for the Appellant. The proviso (iv) to Section 2(2)(b) cannot be an empty formality. It should be an effective right available to a detenu, so as to enable him to assail the order of his preventive detention. A detenu may be advised not to raise a challenge to his order of detention, while it subsists under the stringent conditions of Section 12A, on account of the fact that his remedy would be wider and the grounds available would be far more, when the order of detention is limited to the scope of Section 3 of the COFEPOSA Act. Illustratively it may be mentioned, that on passing of an order of detention Under Section 3 of the COFEPOSA Act, a detenu must be communicated the grounds on which the detention order was made within five days, and in exceptional circumstances (for reasons to be recorded in writing), within fifteen days of the passing of the order of detention (refer to Section 3(3) of the COFEPOSA Act).[22]

4. Accordingly, non-maintenance of the aforesaid procedural parameters would be a justifiable ground to assail the order of detention. Additionally, the grounds on which an order of detention has been passed Under Section 3 of the COFEPOSA Act, have to be furnished to the detenue. The non-communication of the grounds could constitute the basis to assail an order of detention. In case the grounds furnished to the detenu are either vague or irrelevant, and even if they can be shown to be patently false and incorrect, a detenu can successfully challenge an order of his preventive detention. A detenu can also assail an order of his detention, if he is in a position to establish, that the grounds of his detention had not been recorded and signed before the order of detention was passed.[22]

5. The above grounds are not available, in case a declaration is issued (as in the instant case), Under Section 12A of the COFEPOSA Act, wherein it is not essential to furnish grounds of detention to the detenue (refer to Section 12A(5) of the COFEPOSA Act). In case an order of detention is passed Under Section 3 of the COFEPOSA Act, the Government ordering the detention, has to make a reference to the Advisory Board within five weeks (in terms of Section 8(b) of the COFEPOSA Act). On receipt of a reference from the Government, the Advisory Board has to submit a report within eleven weeks from the date of detention (Under Section 8(c) of the COFEPOSA Act). And, an order passed by the Advisory Board opining that there was "... no sufficient cause for the detention of the person concerned..." has to be released forthwith (Under Section 8(f) of the COFEPOSA Act). A detenu whose order of detention has been passed only Under Section 3, without

there being a declaration Under Section 12A of the COFEPOSA Act, would therefore be entitled to seek revocation of an order of detention, if the procedure contemplated Under Section 8 was not complied with, and/or even if the detenu was not released, despite the opinion expressed by the Advisory Board, that the order of detention was not passed on sufficient cause. Or even if it can be shown that the grounds of detention are vague, irrelevant, false or incorrect. None of these grounds are available to a detenu, where a declaration has been issued Under Section 12A of the COFEPOSA Act. The substantive challenge to an order of preventive detention when the order of detention is limited to the scope of Section 3 of the COFEPOSA Act, are far greater. This, because after the declaration Under Section 12A of the COFEPOSA Act, the challenge is only on technical grounds of violation of procedure Under Section 12A of the COFEPOSA Act, as expressed above.[22]

6. In the facts and circumstances of the present case, it is apparent, that the order of detention Under Section 3 of the COFEPOSA Act was passed on 11.6.1976. Immediately after the passing of the aforesaid order, on the same day, the Government of Gujarat issues a declaration Under Section 12A, with reference to the detention of the Appellant. Again, on the lifting of the emergency on 21.3.1977, the declaration Under Section 12A ceased to be operative, with reference to the detention of the Appellant. At the beginning of the order of detention, and at the time of revocation thereof, whilst the detention order subsisted only within the limited scope of Section 3 of the COFEPOSA Act read with Section 12A thereof, there was really no occasion for the Appellant to assail the same thereafter, on any of the grounds as may have been available to him.[23]

7. The Court was satified that in the facts and circumstances of this case, specially the position highlighted by the learned Counsel for the Appellant, as has been noticed hereinabove, the Appellant had no occasion whatsoever to challenge to the order of his detention, on the grounds available to him, while the detention order subsisted under the limited scope of Section 3 of the COFEPOSA Act read with Section 12A thereof after 21.3.1977, as the order Under Section 3 could not have been the subject matter of challenge as the detenu was released on the same day.[24]

8. In the present controversy, the Appellant had no opportunity whatsoever to assail the order of his detention, after his release. As soon as the declaration Under Section 12A of the COFEPOSA Act was revoked, the Appellant was ordered to be released. His release undoubtedly was a

release from detention Under Section 3 of the COFEPOSA Act. The factual position taken into consideration in Attorney General for India and Ors. v. Amratlal Prajivandas and Ors., as highlighted in paragraph 41, in the Court's considered view, would clearly not be applicable to the controversy in hand.[26]

9. The Court was even otherwise persuaded to accept the contention of the Appellant, to enable him to raise a challenge to the order of his detention, for the simple reason, that three of his brothers who raised such a challenge, to the order of their preventive detention, were successful in having the same set aside. The Appellant is possibly similarly situated as his three brothers, and if it is so, he should have the same right as was availed of by his three brothers.[27]

10. In the above view of the matter, the Court was of the view, that the determination rendered by the High Court in not allowing the Appellant to raise a challenge to the order of his detention dated 11.6.1976, was wholly unjustified. The order passed by the High Court is therefore liable to be set aside. The same was accordingly hereby set aside. The Appellant was relegated back to the High Court, so as to enable him to press his claim, on the grounds as may be available to him (to assail the order of his detention dated 11.6.1976). It is only after the determination of the High Court, that it will be open to the authorities to proceed with the action taken against the Appellant Under Section 6 of the SAFEMA Act, and that too, if the Appellant fails in his attempt, to successfully assail the order of his detention.[28]

ppp

SIX

AMRITLAL AND ORS. VS. UNION GOVT. THROUGH SECY. MINISTRY OF FINANCE AND ORS. (07.11.2000 - SC) : MANU/SC/0714/2000

Relative Section:

Narcotic Drugs And Psychotropic Substances Act, 1985 - Section 18, Narcotic Drugs And Psychotropic Substances Act, 1985 - Section 8; Prevention Of Illicit Traffic In Narcotic Drugs And Psychotropic Substances Act, 1988 - Section 3(1)

Hon'ble Judges/Coram : U.C. Banerjee and K.G. Balakrishnan, JJ.

Equivalent Citation: 2000(3)ACR2798(SC), AIR2000SC3675, 2001(1)ALD(Cri)382, 2001 (42) ACC 262, 2001 ALLMR(Cri)745(SC), 2001 (42) ALR 617, 2001(2)BLJ11, IV(2000)CCR279(SC), 2001CriLJ474, 2000(4)Crimes270(SC), 2001(73)ECC10, 2001(2)JLJ190(SC), JT2000(Suppl3)SC178, 2001(II)OLR1,2001(1) RCR (Criminal)81, 2000(7)SCALE597, (2001)1SCC341, [2000]Supp4SCR450, 2001(1)UC142, 2001 (1) UJ555

Number of Pages in the Original Judgment: 3

Case Reference: Binod Singh v. District Magistrate, Dhanbad MANU/ SC/0164/1986; Rivadeneyta Ricardo Agustin v. Govt. of the National Capital Territory of Delhi and Ors. ; Kamarunnissa v. Union of India MANU / SC /0376/1991

Case Note:

Prevention of Illicit Traffic in Narcotic Drugs and Psychotropic Substances Act, 1988-Section 3-Narcotic Drugs and Psychotropic Substances Act, 1985-Sections 8/18-Detention-Validity-Record depicts-Grounds of detention communicated to appellant-Within stipulated time-By subsequent order detention confirmed-High Court dismissed petition-Must be cogent material before officer-To Passing detention order-Not ipse dixit-Before passing detention authority must satisfy-"Likelihood of petitioner being released on bail"-Not "likelihood of moving application for bail". (Para-4,6 and 7)

Facts:

The contextual facts depict that the appellants were arrested pursuant to the raid conducted by the officers of the Central Bureau of Narcotics leading to the seizure of 132 kgs. of opium and crime No. 22/96 was registered against them under Sections 8/18 of the Narcotics Drugs and Psychotropic Substances Act, 1985 (for short 'the Act')-The appellants prayed for being released on bail, but the Addl. District Judge, Neemuch, rejected the application. Subsequently however they were detained under Section 3(1) of the Prevention of Illicit Traffic in Narcotic Drugs and Psychotropic Substances Act, 1988 (for short 'the PITNDPS Act') by order dated 5.6.1997. The record depicts that the grounds of detention were communicated to the appellants within the stipulated time and subsequently by order dated 17.8.1997 their detention has been confirmed. The appellants moved the High Court on the ground that it was illegal and invalid as the detaining authority passed the order mechanically and without application of mind and that facts do not justify their detention. In any event the detention was further challenged on the ground of the same being punitive in nature. The Division Bench of the High Court however dismissed the petitions on the ground that the detaining authority had shown awareness of the petitioners being in the custody and had also communicated the compelling reasons 'by hinting at the likelihood of their enlarging on bail'. The Division Bench of the High Court while dealing with the matter did take into consideration the factum of the two other persons connected with the occurrence being

released on bail and, as such, the detaining authority was not oblivious of
the petitioners' custody and had also provided compelling reasons under
Section 3(1) of the Act[2]

Held, while allowing the appeal

1. In Agustin's decision (supra) this Court also placed strong reliance on
    an earlier but oft-cited decision of this Court in Binod Singh v. District
    Magistrate, Dhanbad MANU/SC/0164/1986 : 1986CriLJ1959 wherein it
    was held that if a person is in custody and there is no imminent
    possibility of his being released therefrom, the power of detention should
    not ordinarily be exercised. This Court held that there must be cogent
    materials before the officer passing the detention order that the detenu
    is likely to be released on bail. The inference must be drawn from the
    available material on record and must not be the ipse dixit of the officer
    passing the order of detention. It is in this perspective as above, that the
    recording of the concerned officer in the matter under reference ought
    to be noticed and the same reads as below:-[4]

Even though prosecution proceedings under Narcotic Drugs and
Psychotropic Substances Act, 1985 have been initiated against Shri Amritlal
I am satisfied that there is compelling necessity in view of the likelihood of
his moving an application for bail and in the event of his being granted bail,
the likelihood of his indulging in illicit traffic in narcotic drugs as is evident
from the trend of his activities, to detain him under the Prevention of Illicit
Traffic in Narcotic Drugs and Psychotropic Substances Act, 1988.

2. It is this reasoning which the learned advocate contended that the
High Court should have held to be completely erroneous in the matter of
being the basis of an order of detention.[5]

3. The requirement as noticed above in Binod Singh's case, (supra) that
there is 'likelihood of the petitioners being released on bail' that however
is not available in the reasonings as provided by the concerned officer. The
reasoning available is the 'likelihood of his moving an application for bail'
which is different from 'likelihood to be released on bail'. This reasoning, in
our view, is not sufficient compliance with the requirements as laid down.[6]

4. The emphasis however, in Binod Singh's case (supra) that before
passing the detention order the concerned authority must satisfy himself of
the likelihood of the petitioner being released on bail and that satisfaction
ought to be reached on cogent material. Available cogent material is the

likelihood of having a bail application moved in the matter but not obtaining a bail order.[7]

5. On the wake of the aforesaid, we do not feel inclined to record our concurrence with the order of detention passed in the matter. As such the same is quashed. The appeals are disposed of accordingly.[8]

ନ୍ଦ୍ନ

SEVEN

R. PAULSAMY VS. UNION OF INDIA (UOI) AND ORS. (14.05.1999 - SC) : MANU/SC/0363/1999

Relative Section:

Constitution Of India - Article 32; Prevention Of Illicit Traffic In Narcotic Drugs And Psychotropic Substances Act, 1988 - Section 12, Prevention Of Illicit Traffic In Narcotic Drugs And Psychotropic Substances Act, 1988 - Section 3(1)

Hon'ble Judges/Coram: G.T. Nanavati and S.N. Phukan, JJ.

Equivalent Citation: 1999(2)ACR1511(SC), AIR1999SC2004, 1999 (39) ACC 292, 1999CriLJ2897, 1999 (3)Crimes50(SC),1999(82)ECR657(SC), JT1999(4)SC16, (1999)123(3)PLR503, 1999(3)SCALE618, (1999) 4SCC415, [1999]3SCR736, 1999(2)UJ995

Number of Pages in the Original Judgment: 3

Case Reference:

Mrs. Venmathi Selvam v. State of Tamil Nadu and Anr. MANU/SC/0398/1998

Case Note:

Held: Detention - Trafficking in Narcotic Drugs--Representation against Detention--Delay in considering--If the delay (even if short) in considering the detenu's representation against his detention is unexplained, such delay becomes unreasonable and vitiates the detention order--ratio of Supreme Court judgment in the case of Venmathi Selvam v. State of Tamil Nadu & Anr. In the present case, the order calling for comments of the Sponsoring Authority (which led to the delay), was not passed by any of the officers empowered by the orders of the Finance Minister dated 7.7.1995. Therefore, the representation was dealt with in a routine manner and there was no application of mind by the competent officer as to whether it was necessary to call for comments of the Sponsoring Authority. The delay from 28.10.1998 to 10.11.1998, being uncalled for, has to be regarded as unreasonable, and, therefore, the detention order is quashed. "..........though the representation was received on 28.10.1998, comments of Sponsoring Authority were called for on 29.10.1998 which were received on 10.11.1998. From the records we find that the order calling for comments of the Sponsoring Authority was not passed, by any of the Officers empowered by the..........orders of the Minister dated 7th July, 1995. Therefore, we hold that the representation was dealt with in a routine manner and there was no application of mind by the competent officer as to whether it was necessary to call for comments of the Sponsoring Authority. In other words, this delay from 28.10.1998 to 10.11.1998 being uncalled for has to be regarded as unreasonable, and, therefore, fatal in view of the ratio laid down by this Court in Venmathi Selvam.......... We, therefore, make the rule absolute, quash and set aside the impugned order of detention and direct that detenue be released forthwith unless he is required to be kept in jail in connection with some other case."

Disposition: In Favour of Accused

Facts:

1. This writ petition has been filed by the detenu under Article 32 of the Constitution of India. The Joint Secretary to the Government of India, Ministry of Finance, Department of Revenue who was empowered under Section 3(1) of the Prevention of Illicit Traffic in Narcotic Drugs and Psychotropic Substances Act, 1988 (for short the Act), being satisfied from the records that it is necessary to prevent the detenu from engaging in illicit trafficking in narcotic drugs in future, passed the order of detention on 28th September, 1998. On the same day grounds of detention were issued and the detenue was informed that he could make a representation against the order of his detention, to the Detaining Authority and/or the Central

Government addressed to the Detaining Authority or to the Secretary to the Government , of India, Ministry of Finance, Department of Revenue. On 26.10.1998 the detenu sent a representation addressed to (1) the Advisory Board. (2) the Secretary to the Government of India, Ministry of Finance and (3) the Detaining Authority.

2. In the counter affidavit dated 11.05.99 filed on behalf of the Union of India i.e. respondent No. 1 it has been stated that the said representation was received in the office on 28.10.1998 and comments from the Sponsoring Authority were called for by letter dated 29.10.98 and the same were received on 10.11.98. The representation along with comments was submitted to the Secretary of the Ministry of Finance on 11.11.98 which was rejected on 12.11.98 after due consideration and detenue was informed by letter dated 13.11.98 which was received by the detenu on 18.11.98. In the counter affidavit the order dated 7th July, 1995 issued by the Minister of Finance has been annexed and we find that power of revocation of detention orders under Section 12 of the Act has been delegated to the Secretary or Additional Secretary or Joint Secretary (Narcotics/in the Ministry of Finance (Department of Revenue), Government of India.

Held, while allowing the appeal

Examining the present case in hand, in the light of the ratio laid down above, we find that though the representation was received on 28.10.1998, comments of Sponsoring Authority were called for on 29.10.1998 which were received on 10.11.1998. From the records we find that the order for calling for comments of the Sponsoring Authority was not passed by any of the Officers empowered by the above orders of Minister dated 7th July, 1995. Therefore, we hold that the representation was dealt with in a routine manner and there was no application of mind by the competent officer as to whether it was necessary to call for comments of the Sponsoring Authority.In other words, this delay from 28.10.98 to 10.11.98 being uncalled for has to be regarded as unreasonable and, therefore, fatal in view of the ratio laid down by this Court in Venmathi Selvam (Mrs.) (supra).We, therefore, make the rule absolute, quash and set aside the impugned order of detention and direct that detenu be released forthwith unless he is required to be kept in jail in connection with some other case. [6]

ppp

EIGHT

KAMLESHKUMAR ISHWARDAS PATEL VS. UNION OF INDIA (UOI) AND ORS. (17.04.1995 – SC) : MANU/SC/0732/ 1995

Relative Section:

Conservation Of Foreign Exchange And Prevention Of Smuggling Activities Act, 1974 - Section 11, Section 11(1), Section 2, Section 3,Section 3(1), Section 3(2);

Constitution Of India - Article 22,Article 22(4),Article 22(5);

General Clauses Act 1897 - Section 1,Section 21;

National Security Act, 1980 - Section 3,Section 3(2),Section 3(3),Section 3(4),Section 8,Section 8(1); Prevention Of Blackmarketing And Maintenance Of Supplies Of Essential Commodities Act, 1980 - Section 12; Prevention Of Illicit Traffic In Narcotic Drugs And Psychotropic Substances Act, 1988 - Section 12, Prevention Of Illicit Traffic In Narcotic Drugs And Psychotropic Substances Act, 1988 - Section 3

Hon'ble Judges/Coram: A.M. Ahmadi, C.J., S.C. Agrawal, S.P. Bharucha, K.S. Paripoornan and S.V. Manohar, JJ.

Equivalent Citation:1995 (32) ACC 461, IV(1995)CCR74(SC), 1995(4)Crimes484(SC),1995(3) Crimes 26(SC), 1996(53)ECC123, 1995(59)ECR168(SC), JT1995(3)SC639, 1995(2)RCR(Criminal)276, 1995(2)SCALE681, (1995) 4SCC 51, [1995]3SCR279

Number of Pages in the Original Judgment: 18

Case Reference:

Amir Shad Khan v. L. Hmingliana, MANU/SC/0440/1991; State of Bombay v. Atma Ram Shridhar Vaidya, MANU/SC/0015/1951; Jayanarayan Sukul v. State of W.B., MANU/SC/0040/1969; Ibrahim Bachu Bafan v. State of Gujarat, MANU/SC/0072/1985; Haradhan Saha v. State of W.B., MANU/SC/ 0419/1974; John Martin v. State of W.B. MANU/SC/0136/1975; Kavita v. State of Maharashtra, MANU/SC/0668/1981; Masuma v. State of Maharashtra, MANU/SC/0226/1981; Sat Pal v. State of Punjab, MANU/SC/0495/1981; Rattan Singh v. State of Punjab, MANU/SC/0696/1981; Abdul Karim v. State of W.B., MANU/SC/0059/1969; Pankaj Kumar Chakrabarty v. State of W.B., MANU/SC/0052/1969; Santosh Anand v. Union of India, ; Raj Kishore Prasad v. State of Bihar, MANU/SC/0098/1982

Case Note:

Preventive Detention - Representation--Fundamental Rights--Procedural Safeguards--Detenu has the right to make a representation to the authority passing the order of detention, and the said authority is obliged to consider the same. Failure to do so will result in the denial of the right of the detenu to make representation against the order of detention--Constitution of India, Art. 22(5); COFEPOSA, 1974; Prevention of Illicit Traffic in Narcotic Drugs & Psychotropic Substances Act, 1988.

Facts:

The question is whether an officer especially empowered by the Central Govt. or a State Govt. to pass an order for preventive detention is required to consider the representation submitted by the detenu.

Held:

1. Preventive detention--Constitution of India, Art. 22(5)--Representation by the detenu--Since the purpose of a representation by the detenu is to get relief at the earliest opportunity, it has to be made to an authority which can revoke the detention order and set him free. The authority that has made the order can also revoke it. This power of the order-making authority is recognised by S. 21 of the General Clauses Act, 1897. The detenu can, therefore, make a representation to the officer empowered to pass the detention order, as also to any other authority who is empowered by law to

revoke the order of detention. The right to make representation also means the right of the person detained, to be informed of the right to make such a representation.

2. Preventive Detention--Conservation of Foreign Exchange and Prevention of Smuggling Activities Act, 1974 (COFEPOSA) and Prevention of Illicit Traffic in Narcotic Drugs & Psychotropic Substances Act, 1988 (PIT NDPS Act)--Representation by detenu--Under these enactments also, the detenu has the right to make a representation to the officer passing the detention order, and the said officer is obliged to consider the representation. Failure on his part to do so, results in denial of the right to the detenu to make a representation against the detention order. "............The power of revocation that is conferred on the Central Government and the State Government under clauses (a) and (b) of sub-section (1) of Section 11 of the COFEPOSA Act and Section 12 of the PIT NDPS Act is in addition to the power of revocation that is available to the authority that has made the order of detention. This is ensued by the words "without prejudice to the provisions of Section 21 of the General Clauses Act, 1897 (10 of 97)" in sub-section (1) of both of provisions."

3.Preventive Detention--Fundamental Rights--Procedural Safeguards--Personal Liberty--Importance of procedural safeguards--Whatever be the harmful consequences of the activities allegedly indulged in by the detenus, the Courts are bound to ensure that the procedural safeguards meant for enforcing the fundamental rights of the people, particularly the right to personal liberty, are not denied to the detenus. "............We are not unmindful of the harmful consequences of the activities in which the detenus art alleged to be involved. But while discharging our constitutional obligation to enforce the fundamental rights of the people, more especially the right to personal liberty, we cannot allow ourselves to be influenced by these considerations. It has been said that history of liberty is the history of procedural safeguards. The framers of the Constitution, being aware that preventive detention involves a serious encroachment on the right to personal liberty, took care to incorporate, in clauses (4) and (5) of Article 22, certain minimum safeguards for the protection of persons sought to be preventively detained. These safeguards are required to be "jealously watched and enforced by the Court". Their rigour cannot be modulated on the basis of the nature of the activities of a particular person."

ᎮᎮᎮ

NINE

GRACY VS. STATE OF KERALA AND ORS. (15.02.1991 - SC) : MANU/SC/0264/1991

Relative Section:

Constitution Of India - Article 22, Constitution Of India - Article 22(5), Constitution Of India - Article 32; Prevention Of Illicit Traffic In Narcotic Drugs And Psychotropic Substances Act, 1988 - Section 10(2), Prevention Of Illicit Traffic In Narcotic Drugs And Psychotropic Substances Act, 1988 - Section 3, Prevention Of Illicit Traffic In Narcotic Drugs And Psychotropic Substances Act, 1988 - Section 8(c), Prevention Of Illicit Traffic In Narcotic Drugs And Psychotropic Substances Act, 1988 - Section 9(f)

Hon'ble Judges/Coram: B.C. Ray, L.M. Sharma and J.S. Verma, JJ.

Equivalent Citation: AIR1991SC1090,1991(Suppl.)AC25,1991(1)Crimes552(SC),1991(33)ECC125, 1991 (54)ELT161(S.C.), JT1991(1)SC371, 1991(I)OLR368, 1991(I)OLR(SC)368, 1991(2)PLJR1, 1991(1) SCALE 211, (1991)2SCC1, [1991]1SCR421, 1991(1)ShimLC324

Number of Pages in the Original Judgment: 5

Case Reference:

John Martin v. State of West Bengal, MANU/SC/0136/1975; S.K. Sekawat v. State of West Bengal, MANU/ SC/0081/1974; K.M. Abdulla Kunhi and B.L. Abdul Khadar v. Union of India and Ors. MANU/SC/0511/1991 ; Sk. Abdul Karim and Ors. v. State of West Bengal MANU/SC/0059/1969; Pankaj Kumar

Chakraborty and Ors. v. State of West Bengal MANU/SC/0052/1969; Shayamal Chakraborty v. The Commissioner of Police, Calcutta and Anr. MANU/SC/0058/1969; B. Sundar Rao and Ors. v. State of Orissa MANU/SC/0070/1971; Haradhan Saha and Anr. v. State of West Bengal and Ors. MANU/SC/0419/1974

Case Note:

Criminal - detention - Sections 3, 9 and 10 of Prevention of Illicit Traffic in Narcotic Drugs and Psychotropic Substances Act, 1988 and Article 22 (5) of Constitution of India - petition to quash Order of detention passed under Section 3 and Order of its confirmation passed under Section 9 (f) read with Section 10 (2) - Apex Court observed detenu's right to have representation considered by Government under Article 22 (5) is independent of consideration of detenue's case and his representation by Advisory Board - there was no independent consideration of detenue's representation by Central Government at any time - there has been breach by Central Government of its duty under Article 22 (5) to consider and decide representation independently of Advisory Board's opinion - Order of detention as well as Order of its confirmation passed by Central Government quashed - petition allowed

Facts:

1. This writ petition under Article 32 of the Constitution of India is by the mother of the detenu Noor alias Babu to quash the detention order F. No. 801/1/90 PITNDPS dated 25.1.1990 passed under Section 3 of the Prevention of Illicit Traffic in Narcotic Drugs and Psychotropic Substances Act, 1988 (in short 'PITNDPS Act') and the order of confirmation F. No. 801/1/90 PITNDPS dated 24.4.1990 passed under Section 9(f) read with Section 10(2) of the PITNDPS Act, by the Central Government directing detention of the detenu for a period of two years w.e.f. 30.1.1990. The only argument advanced in support of this writ petition is infraction of Article 22(5) of the Constitution of India. The facts material for the point raised are stated hereafter.

2. The detenu was arrested from his family estate at Kochuveetil House, Kuthugal, Udumpanchola Taluk, Idikki District, Kerala on 19.10.1989 on the accusation that he and his brothers were involved in extensive illicit cultivation of ganja plants (Cannabis Sativa) in violation of the provisions of Narcotic Drugs and Psychotropic Substances Act, 1985 (in short 'NDPS Act'), He was produced before the Judicial Magistrate who rejected his bail application. The Sessions Judge also rejected the bail application once but late: granted conditional bail. Thereafter, the detention order dated 25.1.1990

was served on the detenu on 30.1.1990. It was stated therein that even though prosecution of the detenu was likely to be initiated under the Narcotic Drugs & Psychotropic Substances Act, there was likelihood of the detenu indulging in cultivation and production of narcotic drugs (ganja) on the detenu being released on bail on account of which there was compelling necessity to detain him under the PITNDPS Act. The detenu was informed that he had a right to make representation to the detaining authority, Central Government and the Central Advisory Board against the detention order. The mode of address of the representation to the Central Government and the Central Advisory Board was also indicated in the detention order along with the grounds of detention in accordance with Article 22(5) of the Constitution of India. The detenu's case was referred by the Central Government to the Central Advisory Board on 2.3.1990. During pendency of the reference before the Advisory Board, the detenu made his representation on 24.3.1990 and addressed it to the Advisory Board. The Advisory Board considered the reference relating to the detenu made by the Central Government and also the detenu's representation submitted to it. The Advisory Board gave the opinion that there was sufficient cause to justify his preventive detention. The Central Government then made the order dated 24.4.1990 confirming his detention and directed that the detenu Noor alias Babu be detained for a period of two years w.e.f. 30.1.1990.

Held, while allowing the appeal

1. It being settled that the aforesaid dual obligation of consideration of the detenu's representation by the Advisory Board and independently by the detaining authority flows from Article 22(5) when only one representation is made addressed to the detaining authority, there is no reason to hold that the detaining authority is relieved of this obligation merely because the representation is addressed to the Advisory Board instead of the detaining authority and submitted to the Advisory Board during pendency of the reference before it. It is difficult to spell out such an inference from the contents of Article 22(5) in support of the contention of the learned Solicitor General. The contents of Article 22(5) as well as the nature of duty imposed thereby on the detaining authority support the view that so long as there is a representation made by the detenu against the order of detention, the aforesaid dual obligation under Article 22(5) arises irrespective of the fact whether the representation is addressed to the detaining authority or to the Advisory Board or to both. The mode of address is only a matter of form which cannot whittle down the requirement of the Constitutional mandate

in Article 22(5) enacted as one of the safeguards provided to the detenu in case of preventive detention.[9]

2. We are, therefore, unable to accept the only argument advanced by the learned Solicitor General to support the detention. On this conclusion, it is not disputed that there has been a breach by the Central Government of its duty under Article 22(5) of the Constitution of India to consider and decide the representation independently of the Advisory Board's opinion. The order of detention dated 25.1.1990 as well as the order dated 24.4.1990 of its confirmation passed by the Central Government are, therefore, quashed. This shall not, however, affect the detenu's prosecution for the alleged offence and it shall also not be construed as a direction to release him in case he is in custody as a result of refusal of bail. The writ petition is allowed, accordingly.[10]

ppp

TEN

P.U. Abdul Rahiman vs. Union of India (UOI) and Ors. (01.11.1990 - SC) : MANU/SC/0077/1991

Relative Section:

Constitution Of India - Article 22(5); Prevention Of Illicit Traffic In Narcotic Drugs And Psychotropic Substances Act, 1988 - Section 10(1), Prevention Of Illicit Traffic In Narcotic Drugs And Psychotropic Substances Act, 1988 - Section 3(1)

Hon'ble Judges/Coram: T.K. Thommen, K.N. Saikia and R.M. Sahai, JJ.

Equivalent Citation: AIR1991SC336, 1991CriLJ430, 1991(1)PLJR65, 1991Supp(2)SCC274

Number of Pages in the Original Judgment:3

Case Reference:

M. Ahamedkutty v. Union of India, MANU/SC/0427/1990;

Abdul Sattar Abdul Kadar Shaikh v. Union of India, MANU/SC/0425/1990

Case Note:

Narcotics - Detention - Section 3(1) of Prevention of Illicit Traffic in Narcotic Drugs and Psychotropic Substances Act, 1988 - Present appeal filed against order whereby detained under Section 3(1) of Act - Held, bail application and bail order were vital materials for consideration - If those were not considered satisfaction of detaining authority itself would have been impaired - If those had been considered, they would be documents relied on by detaining authority though not specifically mentioned to order of detention - Those ought to have formed part of documents supplied to detenu with grounds of detention - Without them grounds themselves could not be said to have been complete - Therefore it amounted to denial of detenu's right to make effective representation - Therefore rendering continued detention of detenu illegal and entitling detenu to be set at liberty - Therefore set aside impugned orders and detenu shall be released and appeal allowed

Facts:

1. The appellant had been arrested on 4-6-1988 under the Narcotic Drugs and Psychotropic Substances Act, 1985. On 9-6-1988 he had moved an application before the Judicial First Class 'Magistrate, Kasargod for bail. That application was rejected. On 10-6-1988 the appellant moved an application for bail, as C.M. P. No. 104/88, before the District & Sessions Judge, Kasarg6d. On 17-6-1988 the appellant was released on bail subject to certain conditions. In the two applications for bail the appellant had specifically stated that he had retracted from the statement made by him. The co-accused, who had also made a statement, had retracted from his statement.[4]

2. On 3-3-1989 the appellant was, pursuant to order dated 13-2-89, arrested and detained. In the grounds of detention there is a specific reference to the appellant's application for bail which was rejected by the Judicial First Class Magistrate, and to the subsequent grant of bail by the Sessions Court.[5]

Held, while allowing the appeal

1. The principle stated by this Court in Abdul Sattar Abdul Kadar Shaik v. Union of India MANU/SC/0425/1990 : (1990)1SCC480 with regard to the irrelevant documents sought by the detenu, has no relevance to a case such as this, the facts of which are squarely covered by the decision in M. Ahamedkutty v. Union of India MANU /SC/0427/1990 : 1990(47)ELT188(SC) .[9]

2. Accordingly, we set aside the judgment under appeal and the impugned orders of detention and declaration. The detenu shall be released at once.[10]

3. The appeal is allowed in the above terms. No costs.[11]

ppp

ELEVEN

SUSHANTA KUMAR BANIK VS. STATE OF TRIPURA AND ORS. (30.09.2022 - SC) : MANU/SC/1262/2022

Relative Section:

Code of Criminal Procedure, 1973 (CrPC); Narcotic Drugs And Psychotropic Substances Act, 1985 - Section 19, Section 21(B), Section 22(b),Section 22(C), Section 24,Section 27A,Section 29, Section 37, Section 37(1); Prevention Of Illicit Traffic In Narcotic Drugs And Psychotropic Substances Act, 1988 - Section 3, Prevention Of Illicit Traffic In Narcotic Drugs And Psychotropic Substances Act, 1988 - Section 3(1)

Hon'ble Judges/Coram: U.U. Lalit, C.J.I., S. Ravindra Bhat and J.B. Pardiwala, JJ

Equivalent Citation: 2022(240)AIC236, AIR2022SC4715, 2022 (2) ALD(Crl.) 929 (SC), 2023 (122) ACC 285, 2022 (3) ALT (Crl.) 251 (A.P.), 2023(2)BomCR(Cri)180, 134(2022)CLT928, 2022/INSC/1053, 2022(4)J.L.J.R.318, 2022(4)PLJR357, 2023(1)RCR(Criminal)432

Number of Pages in the Original Judgment: 11

Case Reference:

Ashok Kumar v. Delhi Administration and Ors. MANU/SC/0052/1982; Sk. Nizamuddin v. State of West Bengal MANU/SC/0080/1974; Suresh Mahato v. The District Magistrate, Burdwan and Ors. MANU/SC/ 0433/1974; Sk. Serajul v. State of West Bengal MANU/SC/0211/1974; Bhawarlal Ganeshmalji v. State of Tamil Nadu and Ors. MANU/SC/0394/1978; Shafiq Ahmad v. District Magistrate, Meerut and Ors. MANU/SC/0491/1989; Ashadevi v. K. Shivraj and Ors. MANU/SC/0057/1978

Case Note:

Narcotics - Detention - Legality - Section 37 of Narcotic Drugs and Psychotropic Substances Act, 1985 - Present appeal is at the instance of a detenu detained under Section 3(1) of the Prevention of Illicit Traffic in Narcotic Drugs and Psychotropic Substances Act, 1988 ('PIT NDPS Act') and is directed against the judgment and order passed by the High Court by which the High Court rejected the writ application filed by the Appellant herein questioning the legality and validity of the detention order passed by the Government of Tripura and thereby affirming the order of detention - Whether High Court rightly rejected the writ application thereby affirming the order of preventive detention?

Facts:

The order of preventive detention came to be passed essentially on the ground that in the past two First Information Reports (FIR) were registered against the Appellant herein for the offences punishable Under Sections 22(b)/22(C)/29 and 21(B) reply of the Narcotic Drugs and Psychotropic Substances Act, 1985 ('NDPS Act, 1985') and is a habitual offender. The first FIR is dated 05.11.2019 and the second FIR is dated 25.04.2021. At the end of the investigation of the FIR dated 05.11.2019, the charge sheet came to be filed and the trial is pending as on date. The investigation so far as the FIR dated 25.04.2021 is concerned, the same is shown to have been pending on the date of the proposal. However, what is important to note is that in both the aforesaid cases registered under the NDPS Act, 1985, the Appellant herein was ordered to be released on bail by the Special Court, Tripura. The Appellant questioned the legality and validity of the detention order by filing the Writ Petition in the High Court. The High Court vide the impugned judgment and order rejected the writ application thereby affirming the order of preventive detention. Appellant (detenu) is before this Court with the present appeal.

Held, while allowing the appeal

1. The requisite subjective satisfaction, the formation of which is a condition precedent to passing of a detention order will get vitiated if material or vital facts which would have bearing on the issue and weighed the satisfaction of the detaining authority one way or the other and influence his mind are either withheld or suppressed by the sponsoring authority or ignored and not considered by the detaining authority before issuing the detention order. [26]

2. In the case on hand at the time when the detaining authority passed the detention order, this vital fact, namely, that the Appellant detenu had been released on bail by the Special Court, Tripura despite the rigours of Section 37 of the NDPS Act, 1985, had not been brought to the notice and on the other hand, this fact was withheld and the detaining authority was given to understand that the trial of those criminal cases was pending. [27]

3. The preventive detention is a serious invasion of personal liberty and the normal methods open to a person charged with commission of any offence to disprove the charge or to prove his innocence at the trial are not available to the person preventively detained and, therefore, in prevention detention jurisprudence whatever little safeguards the Constitution and the enactments authorizing such detention provide assume utmost importance and must be strictly adhered to. [28]

4. The impugned judgment and order passed by the High Court is set aside. The order of preventive detention passed by the State of Tripura is quashed and set aside. The Appellant herein is ordered to be released forthwith from custody if not required in any other case. Appeal allowed. [29]

Disposition: In Favour of Accused.

ÞÞÞ

TWELVE

DHARMENDRA SUGANCHAND CHELAWAT AND ORS. VS. UNION OF INDIA (UOI) AND ORS. (09.02.1990 - SC) : MANU/SC/0226/1990

Relative Section:

Constitution Of India - Article 226; Prevention Of Illicit Traffic In Narcotic Drugs And Psychotropic Substances Act, 1988 - Section 3(1), Prevention Of Illicit Traffic In Narcotic Drugs And Psychotropic Substances Act, 1988 - Section 3(1)(a)

Hon'ble Judges/Coram:

B.C. Ray, Kuldip Singh and S.C. Agrawal, JJ.

Equivalent Citation: AIR1990SC1196,1990 (27) ACC 203, 1990CriLJ1232, 1990(1) Crimes634(SC), 1995(59)ECR22(SC),1990(47)ELT181(S.C.),JT1990(1)SC184, 1990(1)RCR(Criminal)446,1990(1)SCALE146,(1990) 1SCC746, [1990]1SCR303

Number of Pages in the Original Judgment: 8

Case Reference:

Dulal Roy v. District Magistrate, Burdwan, MANU/SC/0112/1975 Vijay Kumar v. State of Jammu & Kashmir, MANU/SC/0127/1982; Alijan Mian v. District Magistrate, Dhanbad, MANU/SC/0082/1983; Binod Singh v. District Magistrate, Dhanbad, Bihar, MANU/SC/0164/1986; Smt. Shashi Aggarwal v. State of U.P., MANU/SC/0457/1988; Vijay Kumar v. Union of India MANU/SC/0568/1988; Ramesh Yadav v. District Magistrate, Etah, MANU/SC/0098/1985; Suraj Pal Sahu v. State of Maharashtra, MANU/SC/0223/1986; N. Meera Rani v. Govt. of Tamil Nadu, MANU/SC/0381/1989; Rameshwar Shaw v. District Magistrate, Burdwan, MANU/SC/0041/1963; Masood Alam v. Union of India, MANU/SC/0278/1973; Ramesh Yadav v. District Magistrate Etah & Ors. [1985 (4) SCC 232];Suraj Paul Sahu v. State of Maharashtra & Ors. [1986 (4) SCC 378];N. Meera Rani v. Govt. of Tamil Nadu & Anr. [1989 (4) SCC 418];Rameshwar Shaw v. District Magistrate, Burdwan & Anr. [1964 (4) SCR 921];Masood Alam etc v. UOI & Ors. [1973 (1) SCC 551];Dulal Roy v. District Magistrate Burdwan [1975 (1) SCC 837];Vijay Kumar v. State of J&K & Ors. [1982 (2) SCC 43];Alijan Mian v. District Magistrate Dhanbad & Ors. [1983 (4) SCC 301];Binod Singh v. District Magistrate Dhanbad, Bihar & Ors. [1986 (4) SCC 416];Smt. Shashi Aggarwal v. State of U.P. & Ors. [1988 (1) SCC 436];Vijay Kumar v. UOI [1988 (2) SCC 57]

Case Note:

Detention - Preventive detention--Offences under NDPS Act--Person already under judicial custody--Grounds of detention must show (i) that the detaining authority is aware that the detenu is already under judicial custody, and (ii) that it was satisfied, on the basis of antecedent activities of the detenu, that it is necessary to detain him to prevent him from engaging in prejudicial activities if released from custody.

Facts:

The Appellants were already in Judicial custody for offences punishable under the NDPS Act, when orders for their preventive detention were passed. Their writ petitions challenging the detention orders were dismissed by the Delhi High Court, against which these appeals were filed.

Held:

Detention--Offences under NDPS Act--Person already in Judicial custody--Grounds of detention must show that the detaining authority was aware that the detenu is already under custody and that on account of the antecedent activities of the detenu it was satisfied that it is necessary to detain him to prevent him from engaging in prejudicial activities.

1. Detention--Offences under NDPS Act--Person already in Judicial custody with no prospect of release from such custody in the near future--Detention order not sustainable.

❧❧❧

THIRTEEN

SYED FAROOQ MOHAMMAD VS. UNION OF INDIA (UOI) AND ORS. (14.05.1990 - SC) : MANU/SC/0289/1990

Relative Section:

Code of Criminal Procedure, 1973 (CrPC) - Section 82; Code of Criminal Procedure, 1973 (CrPC) - Section 83; Code of Criminal Procedure, 1973 (CrPC) - Section 84; Code of Criminal Procedure, 1973 (CrPC) - Section 85; Conservation Of Foreign Exchange And Prevention Of Smuggling Activities Act, 1974 - Section 3(1), Conservation Of Foreign Exchange And Prevention Of Smuggling Activities Act, 1974 - Section 7; Constitution Of India - Article 166, Constitution Of India - Article 22(5); Customs Act, 1962 - Section 108; Indian Penal Code 1860, (IPC) - Section 302; National Security Act, 1980 - Section 3(2); Prevention Of Illicit Traffic In Narcotic Drugs And Psychotropic Substances Act, 1988 - Section 3(1), Prevention Of Illicit Traffic In Narcotic Drugs And Psychotropic Substances Act, 1988 - Section 7, Prevention Of Illicit Traffic In Narcotic Drugs And Psychotropic Substances Act, 1988 - Section 8

Hon'ble Judges/Coram: B.C. Ray and P.B. Sawant, JJ.

Equivalent Citation: AIR1990SC1597, 1990 (27) ACC 474, 1990CriLJ1622, 1990(2)Crimes619(SC), JT1990(3)SC102, 1990(2)RCR(Criminal)402, (1990)3SCC537, [1990]3SCR240, 1990(2)UJ395

Number of Pages in the Original Judgment: 8

Case Reference:

Binod Singh v. District Magistrate, Dhanbad, Bihar MANU/SC/0164/1986; Suraj Pal Sahu v. State of Maharashtra MANU/SC/0223/1986; Shafiq Ahmad v. District Magistrate, Meerut MANU/ SC/0491 /1989; Bhawarlal Ganeshmalji v. State of Tamil Nadu MANU/SC/0394/1978; T.A. Abdul Rahman v. State of Kerala, MANU/SC/0036/1990; Madan Lal Anand v. Union of India. MANU/SC/0030/1990; Mohinuddin v. District Magistrate, Beed, MANU/SC/0121/1987; Niranjan Singh v. State of Madhya Pradesh, MANU/ SC/0194/1972; Habibullah Khan v. State of West Bengal, MANU/SC/0109/ 1973; Jagdish Prasad v. State of Bihar MANU/SC/0144/1974; Mohd. Alam v. State of West Bengal, MANU/SC/0169/1974

Case Note:

Narcotics - Detention - Section 3(1) of Prevention of Illicit Traffic in Narcotic Drugs and Psychotropic Substances Act, 1988 - Petitioner detained under Section 3 (1) with a view to prevent him from engaging in abetting and transportation of narcotic drug - Petitioner challenged detention Order on ground that detention Order was passed after nearly six months of incident - Further contended that no detention Order against X was passed on same evidence - Further contended that grounds of detention had not been supplied to petitioner and detention Order was passed without application of mind - Facts revealed that detention Order has been made with promptitude considering the relevant and vital facts proximate to the passing of the impugned Order of detention - Held, non-furnishment to detenu bail application and Order passed thereupon did not effect in any manner whatsoever detenu right to make effective representation as these documents were not considered by detaining authority while making detention Order - Detaining authority carefully scrutinised all the relevant documents and facts of the case and arrived at his subjective satisfaction that preventive order of detention of the petitioner is necessary to prevent him from smuggling and transporting contraband goods and as such the impugned order of detention is not at all illegal or bad and the same is not vitiated by non-application of mind or non-consideration of relevant materials - Delay in presenting detention Order was not without reason as revealed that petitioner has intentionally absconded and thereby evaded arrest - Appeal dismissed

Facts:

1. The petitioner, Syed Farooq Mohammad has challenged the order of his detention passed on December 20, 1989 under Section 3(1) of the Prevention of Illicit Traffic in Narcotic Drugs and Psychotropic Substances Act, 1988, and served on him on February 15, 1990. The order of detention was issued by Nisha Sahai Achuthan, Joint Secretary to the Government of India who was specially empowered under Section 3(1) of the Prevention of Illicit Traffic in Narcotic Drugs & Psychotropic Substances Act and it recited that with a view to preventing the petitioner from engaging in abetting and transportation of narcotic drugs, the said Sayyed Farook Mohd. @ Farooq @ Sayyed Farooq Isamuddin @ Anand be detained and kept in custody in the Yervada Central Prison, Pune. The grounds of detention were also served on the same day i.e. February 15, 1990 immediately after his arrest by the Customs Authorities.

2. On July 19, 1989 the staff of the Preventive Collectorate Customs, Bombay impounded two fiat cars bearing Nos. GJV 5440 and MHY 2625. The drivers of the said cars namely Aslam Mohammad Nazir and Mohammad Yakub Sheikh were apprehended. On search of the two cars, 100 packets of brown coloured powder purporting to be narcotic drug of Pakistani origin was found out of the dickers of the cars. The narcotic drug recovered from the dickies of the said cars weighed 100 kgs. and its value in the market is about 2.34 crores. Car No. GJV 5440 belonged to the petitioner-detenu, Syed Farooq Mohammad and the other car No. MHY 2625 belonged to one C.P. Reddy, an Officer of international airport who was also apprehended and his statement Under Section 108 of the Customs Act was recorded. It was revealed from his statement that this car was also used for transporting heroin along with petitioner's car. The statements of Aslam Mohammad Nazir and Mohammad Yakub Sheikh who were apprehended as well as the statement of other person i.e. Mohd. Azam Khan @ Wali Mohd. Khan @ Hameed Khan were also recorded Under Section 108 of the Customs Act by the Customs Officials. From these statements it appeared that these persons were known to the detenu and they used to visit often the hotel 'Fisherman' at World for disco. The detenu i.e. Farooq Mohammad also used to go for disco in the said hotel 'Fisherman' at Worli. It has been stated by Aslam Mohammad Nazir that on July 19, 1989 he was sitting in room No. 106, 2nd Floor, Kali Building near Burtan apartment, Bombay Central (residence of the detenu) along with his friend, Mohd. Yakub Sheikh, driver of the other

car. Hameed also came there to meet Farooq Mohammad. Hameed asked him and Mohd. Yakub Sheikh to go along with him to Kalina. He told them that a truck had come to Kalina with some packets of contraband goods and that they were to take those packets near Jaslok hospital. Thereafter, he took two fiat cars bearing registration Nos. GJV 5440 and MHY 2625 from Farooq. He gave the keys of car No. GJV 5440 to him and car No. MHY 2625 to Mohd. Yakub. Thereafter, they drove those two cars to Kalina as per Hameed's instructions and Hameed led them in a red maruti car bearing No. BLB 7445 where Hameed showed them one truck wherefrom four gunny bags were unloaded and kept in the dickies of the above said two cars. It further appears from his statement that as per Hameed's instructions after the cars were parked near Jaslok Hospital, they handed over the keys of both the cars to Hameed and he told them to contact him again in the evening on telephone No. 367373 of R.K. Hotel. From Farooq place they contacted him over the telephone. Hameed told them to wait there and he was coming there. Thereafter Hameed took them in the Maruti Car to a place near Tejpal Road, Gowalia Tank. There he showed them the same two fiat cars bearing Nos. GJV 5440 and MHY 2625. Hameed gave the keys of the car No. GJV 5440 to him and car No. MHY 2625 to Mohd. Yakub Sheikh and asked them to drive the said two cars following his car. etc. etc.

3. Similar statement was made by Mohd. Yakub Sheikh which was recorded by the Customs Officials. It has also been stated by them that they were told by Hameed that each of them will get Rs. 5,000 as monetary consideration. Yakub also stated that similar jobs have been done by him on 4-5 occasions and he received Rs. 5,000 each time from Hameed. From the statement of Hameed recorded by the Customs Officials, it appears that on July 19, 1989 afternoon he collected two drivers namely Aslam Mohd. Nazir and Mohd. Yakub Sheikh and two fiat cars from Farooq of Bombay Central. This Farooq was introduced to him by Mohd. Nasir, a narcotic drug dealer who is now detained in Rajasthan in connection with a drug case.

4. The detaining authority searched the residence of the detenu on July 20, 1989 but nothing incriminating could be found there from. After recording the statements of these persons and examining and considering the test reports dated October 13, 1989, September 29, 1989 and November 15, 1989 which mentioned that the brown powder contained in those 100 packets is narcotic drug coming within the Narcotic Drugs and Psychotropic Substances Act, the impugned order of detention was made on December 20, 1989 and the petitioner was arrested and detained on service of the order

of detention on February 15, 1990.

5. The challenge to the detention order had been made in the instant writ petition principally on four grounds which are as under:

(1) The impugned order of detention has been passed relying on the incident which is absolutely stale as the incident is dated July 19, 1989 whereas the impugned order has been passed on December 20, 1989.

(2) The statements of the three persons as recorded in the form of statement under Section 108 of the Customs Act came to the respondents on July 20, 1989. The order should have been passed immediately on 20th July, 1989 but the order has been passed on December 20, 1989 i.e. after five months. The impugned order, it is therefore contended, is illegal and has been passed on stale ground.

(3) Since no order of preventive detention has been passed against C.P. Reddy on the same evidence, no order should have been passed against the petitioner as his involvement is of the same nature and to the same extent as that of C.P. Reddy.

(4) Assuming that the order rejecting bail application has been considered though not evident from the grounds of detention supplied, yet the same has not been supplied to the petitioner. This indicates that a relevant document has not been supplied to the petitioner which affected his right of effective representation guaranteed under Article 22(5) of the Constitution. The petitioner after grant of bail by an order of this Court appeared before the respondents and applied for making statement Under Section 108 of the Customs Act. He was arrested and the order of detention was served on him. This material aspect should have been considered before serving the impugned order.

6. As regards the first ground, the counsel for the petitioner has vehemently urged before this Court that the statements of the two persons i.e. Aslam Mohd. Nazir and Mohd. Yakub Sheikh the drivers of the said two cars handed over by the petitioner for carrying narcotic drugs and also the statement of Hameed, did not implicate the petitioner in the transportation and smuggling of the drugs and as such there was non-application of mind on the part of the detaining authority in clamping the order of detention on the petitioner. The impugned order of detention is, therefore, vitiated by non-application of mind. The learned Counsel referred to certain portions of the statements recorded by the Customs Officials Under Section 108 of the Customs Act and contended with great emphasis that there was nothing to say that the petitioner was implicated in the smuggling or transportation of

the heroin which has been seized from the dickies of the two cars.

7. This contention of the learned Counsel is totally devoid of merit in as much as the statements of these three persons as recorded by the Customs Officials Under Section 108 of the Customs Act clearly implicate the petitioner who knowing fully that these two cars will be used for the purpose of transportation of prohibited drugs i.e. heroin and for selling of the same, handed over the keys of the two cars to the said two drivers who were sitting at his residence with Hameed on the asking of Hameed for carrying the contraband goods. In these circumstances, it is meaningless to argue that the statements of these three persons did not implicate the petitioner. All the aforesaid three persons were well known to the petitioner and were sitting at the petitioner's residence, they were given the keys of the petitioner's car as well as the keys of the car of C.P. Reddy which was brought to his garage for repairs by one Ravi Poojari through whom C.P. Reddy sent his car for repairs. The petitioner knowing fully well that these two cars will be used for the purpose of transporting contraband goods i.e. heroin from the truck stationed at Kalina from which four gunny bags containing the said heroin were unloaded and placed in the dickies of these two cars, handed over the keys of the cars. It is also evident from these statements recorded by the Customs Officials that the petitioner along with those three persons used to visit hotel 'Fisherman' for disco regularly and they were well-known to the petitioner. In these circumstances, it is beyond pale of any doubt that the petitioner knowing fully well that these two cars will be used for transporting contraband goods, i.e. heroin, handed over the keys of the cars for the said purpose. Therefore, this challenge is wholly without any basis.

Held, while allowing the appeal

1. In the instant case, the counter-affidavit has been filed by Shri A.K. Roy, Under Secretary to the Government, Ministry of Finance, Department of Revenue, New Delhi although the order of detention was made by Nisha Sahai Achuthan, Joint Secretary to the Government of India, Ministry of Finance. It is evident that the said Under Secretary was dealing with the papers relating to the particular order of detention and he placed those papers before the Minister concerned. In these circumstances, the counter-affidavit filed on behalf of the respondents cannot but be considered and there is no allegation of mala fide or malice or extraneous consideration personally against the detaining authority in making the impugned order of detention. This contention is, therefore, not tenable.[20]

2. In the premises aforesaid we dismiss the writ petition and hold that the impugned order of detention is quite in accordance with law and the same is valid. The observations made herein are confined to this application.[21]

ppp

FOURTEEN

GAZI KHAN VS. STATE OF RAJASTHAN AND ORS. (02.05.1990 - SC) : MANU/SC/0266/1990

Relative Section:

Arms Act 1959 - Section 25; Constitution Of India - Article 166, Constitution Of India - Article 21, Constitution Of India - Article 22(5); Customs Act, 1962 - Section 108

Hon'ble Judges/Coram: S.R. Pandian and K. Jayachandra Reddy, JJ.

Equivalent Citation: AIR1990SC1361, 1990 (27) ACC 468, 1990CriLJ1420, 1990(2)Crimes482(SC), 1990(29)ECC5, JT1990(3)SC28, 1990(3)RCR(Criminal)405, 1990(1)SCALE869, (1990)3SCC459, [1990]2SCR831, 1990(2)ShimLC107, 1990(1)WLN289

Number of Pages in the Original Judgment: 8

Case Reference:

State of Bombay v. Purushottam Jog Naik MANU/SC/0016/1952; Ranjit Dam v. State of West Bengal, MANU/SC/0217/1972; J.N. Roy v. State of West Bengal, MANU/SC/0144/1972 : 1973 SCC 123 MANU/SC/0144/1972; Gulab Mehra v. State of U.P. MANU/SC/0225/1987; State of Gujarat v. Sunil Fulchand Shah, MANU/SC/0473/1988; Madan Lal anand v. Union of India, MANU/SC/0030/1990; Rama Dhondu Borade v. V.K. Saraf, Commr. of Police, MANU/SC/0449/1989; Smt. Shalini Soni v. Union of India, MANU/SC/0227/1980; Shaik Hanif v. State of West Bengal, MANU/SC/0428/1974; Bhut Nath

Mate v. State of West Bengal MANU/SC/0412/1974; Asgar Ali v. District Magistrate, Burdwan and Ors. MANU/SC/0409/1974

Case Note:

Narcotics - Detention - Section 3 (1) of the Prevention of Illicit Traffic in Narcotic Drugs and Psychotropic Substance Act, 1989 - Appellant detained under Section 3 for being illegally involved in business of smuggled 'charas' and heroin and other psychotropic substances - Appeal dismissed by High Court - Hence, present appeal - Appellant contended that detention Order was vitiated as representation was not decided within a reasonable time - Present additional affidavit sworn to by the Commissioner and Secretary on 21.4.1990 also does not whisper any explanation as to why such a delay of 7 days had occurred at the hands of the Assistant Secretary - Set aside impugned order of detention on ground that there was a breach of constitutional obligation as enshrined under Article 22(5) - appeal allowed

Prevention of Illicit Traffic in Narcotic Drugs and Psychotropic Substances Act, 1938 - Section 3(1)--Constitution of India-Article 22(5)-Detention--Affidavit by Dy. SP not dealing with case--Held it is highly deprecated.

This practice of allowing a Police Officer who has not dealt with the case at any point of time at any level and who in the very nature of the case could not have any personal knowledge of the proceedings, to swear the counter and reply affidavits on behalf of the appropriate authorities should be highly deprecated and condemned and the counter and reply affidavits sworn by such officer merit nothing but rejection.

(b) Constitution of India - Article 22(5) and Prevention of Illicit Traffic in Narcotic Drugs and Psychotropic Substances Act, 1988--Section 3--Detention--No explanation for 7 days delay in putting note by Asst. Secretary on comments of District Magistrate--Affidavit filed Dy. SP not worth considering-Held, there is breach of constitutional obligation Under Article 22(5).

There is no explanation for the delay from 3rd to 9th July, 1989, i.e. for 7 days for the Assistant Secretary merely to put up a note on the basis of the comments of the Disirict Magistrate.

The affidavit filed by the Deputy Superintendent of Police is not worth consideration and there is absolutely no explanation for the delay caused at the hands of the Assistant Secretary.

Therefore, for the reasons stated above, we set aside the impugned order of detention on the ground that there is a reach of constitutional obligation as enshrined Under Article 22(5) of the Constitution of India.

Appeal Allowed.

Facts:

4. The detenu Gazi Khan @ Chotia was actively involved in illegal and objectionable activities by organising a group of smugglers and financing them in the activities of smuggling without directly involving himself in such activities. However, the police of Jaisalmer has opened a history sheet showing the indirect involvement of the detenu in such smuggling activities. The modus operandi of the detenu is revealed in the statements recorded under Section 108 of the Customs Act from a number of smugglers who were apprehended in the course of smuggling. On 3.11.1986 the detenu has himself given a statement before the Customs Officer admitting his involvement in smuggling of ready-made garments and bidis. He was suspected in Offence No. 32 dated 30.3.1988 as well in Offence No. 17 dated 17.4.88 under the provisions of the Act as well under Section 25 of the Arms Act. But since no evidence was available incriminating the detenu with those offences no action could be taken. Further the detenu is said to have been involved along with his associates in certain criminal cases registered under the provisions of the Indian Penal Code. The detaining authority on the above materials placed before him has passed this impugned order. The High Court before which he challenged the impugned order detention on various grounds has dismissed the Writ Petition holding that all the contentions did not merit consideration. Hence this appeal.

Held, while allowing the appeal

However, in the same decision it has been pointed out that "what is reasonable dispatch depends on the facts and circumstances of each case and no hard and fast rule can be laid in that regard." We have already expressed that the affidavit filed by the Deputy Superintendent of Police is not worth consideration and there is absolutely no explanation for the delay caused at the hands of the Assistant Secretary.

18. Therefore, for the reasons stated above, we set aside the impugned order of detention on the ground that there is a breach of F constitutional obligation as enshrined under Article 22(5) of the Constitution of India. In the result, the appeal is allowed and the detenu is directed to be set at liberty forthwith.[18]

ppp

FIFTEEN

Ankit Ashok Jalan vs. Union of India (UOI) and Ors. (04.03.2020 - SC) : MANU/SC/0276/2020

Relative Section:

Conservation Of Foreign Exchange And Prevention Of Smuggling Activities Act, 1974 - Section 2(a), Section 2(b), Section 3, Section 3(1), Section 3(2), Section 3(3), Section 7, Section 8, Section 8(b), Section 8(c), Section 8(e), Section 8(f), - Section 9, Section 11, Section 11(1), Section 11(2), Section 13;

Constitution Of India - Article 14, Article 19, Article 21, Article 22, Article 22(4), Article 22(5),Article 32; General Clauses Act 1897 - Section 21;

National Security Act, 1980 - Section 3(3), Section 3(4),Section 8(1); Section 3(1), Section 3(2), Section 7(1); Maintenance of Internal Security Act, 1971; Prevention of Illicit Traffic in Narcotic Drugs and Psychotropic Substances Act, 1988 - Section 12

Hon'ble Judges/Coram: U.U. Lalit, Indu Malhotra and Hemant Gupta, JJ.

Equivalent Citation: AIR2020SC1936, 2020(1)Crimes414(SC), 2020/INSC/266, 2020(3)JCC1517, 2021-1-LW(Crl)173, 2020(2)MLJ(Crl)120, (2020)16SCC127, 2020 (5) SCJ 193, [2020]2SCR1047

Number of Pages in the Original Judgment: 44

Case Reference:

Golam Biswas vs. Union of India (UOI) and Ors. MANU/SC/0752/2015; K.M. Abdulla Kunhi and B.L. Abdul Khader vs. Union of India (UOI) and Ors. and State of Karnataka and Ors. MANU/SC/0511/1991; Ibrahim Bachu Bafan vs. State of Gujarat and Ors MANU/SC/0072/1985; State of Maharashtra and Anr. vs. Sushila Mafatlal Shah and Ors. MANU/SC/0482/1988; Sat Pal vs. State of Punjab and others MANU/SC/0495/1981; Amir Shad Khan and another vs. L. Hmingliana and others MANU/SC/0440/1991; Kamleshkumar Ishwardas Patel vs. Union of India (UOI) and Ors. MANU/SC/0732/1995; The State of Bombay vs. Atma Ram Sridhar Vaidya MANU/SC/0015/1951; Sk. Abdul Karim and Ors. vs. State of West Bengal MANU/SC/0059/1969; John Martin vs. State of West Bengal MANU/SC/0136/1975; Pankaj Kumar Chakrabarty and Ors. vs. The State of West Bengal MANU/SC/0052/1969; Frances Coralie Mullin vs. W.C. Khambra and Ors. MANU/SC/0260/1980; Nagendra Nath Mondal vs. The State of West Bengal MANU/SC/0181/1972; Vimalchand Jawantraj Jain vs. Shri Pradhan and Ors. MANU/SC/0287/1979; Jayanarayan Sukul vs. State of West Bengal MANU/SC/0040/1969; Haradhan Saha vs. The State of West Bengal and Ors. MANU/SC/0419/1974; Khairul Haque v. State of W.B. W.P. No. 246 of 1969; Om Prakash Bahl v. Union of India W.P. No. 845 of 1979

Case Note:

The Joint Secretary to the Government of India, specially empowered under Section 3(1) of the COFEPOSA Act passed the Detention Orders after being satisfied that with a view to prevent the detenues from smuggling goods, abetting the smuggling of goods, and dealing in smuggled goods otherwise than by engaging in transporting or concealing or keeping smuggled goods, in future, it was necessary to make the said Detentions Orders. The cases of the detenues were referred to the Central Advisory Board along with the grounds of detention and relied upon documents. The representation made on behalf of both the detenues, addressed to the Joint Secretary (COFEPOSA), Government of India. The representation was forwarded to the Sponsoring Authority. Said representation as well as the para-wise comments received from the Sponsoring Authority were forwarded to the Central Advisory Board. The Writ Petition preferred on behalf of the detenues was allowed by the High Court on the grounds that when the detenues were in judicial custody and there was no imminent possibility of their release on bail and when not even a bail application was preferred by them, the power of preventive detention ought not to have been exercised; and, that non-placement of relevant material in the form of retraction petition and its non-consideration by the Detaining Authority vitiated the Detention Orders. The High Court thus quashed the Detention Orders and directed that the detenues be released forthwith. The Central Advisory Board recorded that since the Detention Orders were quashed, there was no possibility of proceeding further in the matter. The decision of the High Court was challenged in Criminal Appeal in this Court, which by its Judgment and order set aside the view taken by the High Court. A direction was issued to process the files of the detenues for reference to the Central Advisory Board. After obtaining appropriate approval, the case was referred to the Central Advisory Board stating inter alia that the representation would be considered only after the receipt of the opinion of the Central Advisory Board.

Held, while allowing the appeal:

U.U. Lalit, J.

(i) In terms of Section 8, the report of the Advisory Board is meant only for the consumption of the appropriate Government and apart from the operative part of the report which is to be specified in a separate paragraph as per Sub-section (c), the mandate in terms of Sub-section (e) is to keep the report of the Advisory Board completely confidential. Thus, a specially empowered officer who may have passed the order of detention, by statutory intent is not to be privy to the report nor does the statute contemplate any role for such specially empowered officer at the stage of consideration of the opinion of the Advisory Board. The report of the Advisory Board may provide some qualitative inputs for the appropriate Government but none to the specially empowered officer who acted as the Detaining Authority. If that be so, would a specially empowered officer who had passed the order of detention be bound by what has been laid down by this Court in the decision in K.M. Abdulla Kunhi in the context of the appropriate Government. [23]

(ii) Thus, if the law was now settled that a representation can be made to the specially empowered officer who had passed the order of detention in accordance with the power vested in him and the representation has to be independently considered by such Detaining Authority, the concerned principles adverted to in the decision in K.M. Abdulla Kunhi would not be the governing principles for such specially empowered officer. It must be stated that the discussion in K.M. Abdulla Kunhi was purely in the context where the order of detention was passed by the appropriate Government and not by the specially empowered officer. The principle laid down had therefore to be understood in the light of the subsequent decision rendered by another Constitution Bench of this Court in Kamleshkumar. [25]

(iii) The Detaining Authority ought to have considered the representation independently and without waiting for the report of the Central Advisory Board. The facts in the instant case indicate that the comments of the Sponsoring Authority in respect of the representation were already received by the Detaining Authority. After receipt of letter that the detenues were received in custody, the time for considering the representation started ticking for the Detaining Authority. But the representation was considered and the reason for such delayed consideration was that the report of the Central Advisory Board was awaited. The Detaining Authority was obliged to consider the representation without waiting for the opinion of the Central Advisory Board. Thus, there was no valid explanation for non-consideration of the representation. Therefore, complete inaction on part of the Detaining Authority in considering the representation caused prejudice to the detenues and violated their constitutional rights. [26]

(iv) Since there was complete inaction on part of the Detaining Authority in the present case, to whom a representation was addressed in dealing with the representation, it was held that the constitutional rights of the detenues were violated and the detenues were entitled to redressal on that count. Therefore, the continued detention of the detenues in terms of the Detention Orders to be illegal, invalid and unconstitutional. [28]

Hemant Gupta, J.

(i) Once the detention order had been made by any of the authorities competent to detain in terms of Section 3(1) of the COFEPOSA Act, the representation to seek revocation of the detention order could be considered and decided by the Detaining Authority dehors the decision of the Advisory Board and the acceptance of recommendation by the appropriate Government. The consideration for revocation of a detention order was limited to examining whether the order conforms with the provisions of law whereas the recommendation of the Advisory Board was on the sufficiency of material for detention, which alone was either confirmed or not accepted by the appropriate Government. [51]

(ii) It would be a matter of prudence and propriety for the Detaining Authority to defer the decision on the representation to revoke the detention order, when the matter was being considered by the Advisory Board, consisting of three sitting Judges of the High Court. The consideration of the representation by the Detaining Authority in these circumstances could not be said to be delayed as the representation was received after the matter was referred to the Advisory Board. [52]

Disposition: In Favour of Accused.

❦❦❦

SIXTEEN

BIRENDRA KUMAR RAI VS. UNION OF INDIA (UOI) AND ORS. (03.09.1992 - SC) : MANU/SC/0435/1993

Relative Section:

Arms Act 1959 - Section 25; Constitution Of India - Article 136, Article 22(5);

Motor Vehicles Act, 1988 - Section 207;

Prevention Of Illicit Traffic In Narcotic Drugs And Psychotropic Substances Act, 1988 – Sec. 10(1) to Sec.3(1)

Hon'ble Judges/Coram: Kuldip Singh and N.M. Kasliwal, JJ.

Equivalent Citation: 1992()ACR694(SC), AIR1993SC962, 1992(90) ALJ 1249, 1993 (30) ACC 556, 1993 AWC 385 SC, 1993(1)BLJR219, 1993CriLJ158, 1992(3)Crimes398(SC), 1993(43)ECC81, 1993 GLH (2) 617, JT1992(5)SC264, 1995(5)SCALE210, (1993)1SCC272, [1992]Supp1SCR391

Number of Pages in the Original Judgment: 7

Case Reference: nil

Case Note:

Criminal - detention - Section 25 of Arms Act, Section 207 of Motor Vehicles Act and Sections 3 and 10 of Prevention of Illicit Traffic in Narcotic

Drugs and Psychotropic Substances Act, 1988 - petitioner arrested in connection with offences under Section 25 and Section 207 - petitioner alleged to have been engaged in clandestine business of preparing and selling heroine - petitioner detained for alleged offence - detention challenged - substantive material on record established that petitioner was engaged in illicit purchase, sale, possession and abetting of narcotic drugs - detention Order valid and does not require any interference.

Facts:

2. The petitioner was arrested on 21.11.1990 by Zamania Police in connection with Crime No. 402 of 1990 under Section 25 of the Arms Act and Section 207 of the Motor Vehicles Act. The petitioner was detained in District Jail, Ghazipur in connection with the above case. During the custody of the petitioner in District Jail Ghazipur he was served on 10.12,1990 with a detention order passed by the Joint Secretary to the Government of India, Ministry of Finance, Department of Revenue, New Delhi, under Section 3(1) of the Prevention of Illicit Traffic in Narcotic Drugs and Psychotropic Substance Act, 1988 (hereinafter referred to as the TITNDPS Act, 1988). The petitioner was given the grounds of detention along with the copies of documents relied on by the detaining authority along with the detention order.[2]

3. It was alleged in the grounds of detention that on a secret information the Officers of Varanasi and Delhi units of Narcotic Control Bureau intercepted Shanti Swaroop and A.K. Chaudhary alias P.P. Singh on the night of 12/13th August, 1990 at the Indira Gandhi International Airport (Terminal-II), New Delhi when they reported for boarding Flight No. K.L. 836 to Amsterdam. On search of their baggage, P.P. Singh was found to possess 975 grams of Heroin concealed in the false bottom of his shoulder bag. On the basis of statements and disclosures made by these persons, the house of the petitioner, his father and brothers were searched and 855,250 grams of foreign marked 7 gold biscuits and some incriminating documents were recovered. On search of the petitioner's flat at Varanasi some more documents were recovered. The father and brothers of the petitioner in their statements admitted their involvement in the business of Heroin. Kamla Rai also stated that the petitioner fell into bad company and started preparing Heroin from Opium and the petitioner also joined his brothers in the same trade and from the money earned from the said business the petitioner had purchased one flat at Andheri (Bombay). The statements of the members of the petitioner's family clearly revealed that the petitioner had been engaged

in the clandestine business of preparing and selling Heroin.[3]

4. On 7.11.1990 a complaint was filed against the petitioner and others under the Narcotic Drugs and Psychotropic Substances Act, 1985 (hereinafter referred to as the 'NDPS Act, 1985'). Before any warrant of arrest could be served on the petitioner in respect of the aforesaid case lodged under the Narcotic Drugs & Psychotropic Substances Act, 1985, the petitioner was arrested on 21.11.1990 in the case registered under the Arms Act and the Motor Vehicles Act. He was arrested and detained in District Jail Ghazipur. The petitioner moved an application for bail on 3.12.1990 before the Session Judge in respect of the case under Narcotic Drugs & Psychotropic Substances Act, 1985. The detention order under Section 3(1) of the PITNDPS Act, 1988 was passed by the Joint Secretary to the Government of India on 4.12.1990 and the aforesaid detention order was served along with the grounds of detention on 10.12.1990 while the petitioner was in the custody at District Jail Ghazipur. The petitioner made a representation to the President of India and Joint Secretary to the Government of India on 22.12.1990. The Central Government rejected the representation on 25.1.1991. The petitioner then filed a habeas corpus petition in the Allahabad High Court challenging his detention. There was a difference of opinion between the two Learned Judge of the High Court in the order pronounced on the habeas corpus petition on 23.4.1991. The matter was ultimately heard by the Full Bench of the High Court and the Writ Petition was dismissed by unanimous order dated 21.2.1992. The petitioner aggrieved against the order of the High Court has come before this Court by filing special leave petition under Article 136 of the Constitution.[4]

Held, while allowing the appeal

13. A perusal of the above explanation given by the Union of India explains the time taken in dealing with the representation. The period taken by the postal authorities cannot be attributed to any delay or inaction or callousness on the part of the authorities considering such representation. Now, if we consider the period after 20th April, 1992, it may be noted that some time was taken in wrongly marking the representation to some other branch by the receipt section of the department. However, the representation was received in the concerned section of PITNDPS CELL on 27. 4.1992. 25th and 26th April, 1992 were holidays. Much stress is laid by the Learned Counsel for the Petitioner on the time spent during the period the representation was wrongly marked to some other branch. Mr. Tulsi in this regard submitted that it was due to human error and the period spent in

wrongly marking the representation to some other branch is not a long one, but only five days. We are satisfied with the above submission made by Mr. Tulsi. It was be further noted that this representation was not against the order of detention or any grounds hi support of the detention order, but it was a representation against the declaration made under Section 10(1) of PITNDPS Act, 1988. The period from 27.4.1992 till 27.5.1992 has been explained in detail in the counter affidavit filed before this Court and a perusal of the above explanation shows that the time taken cannot be considered so as to draw an inference of inaction or callousness on the part of the authorities. Thus, we do not find any substance in the second ground of challenge levelled by the petitioner against the detention.[13]

14. Before parting with the case we would like to say that this Court has already laid down the law relating to detentions under the preventive detention laws during the last four decades. If the Government takes care that the detention cases arising under the preventive detention laws are handled by persons fully trained and having experience in such matters, the rights of the citizens can be safeguarded and the precious time of this Court can be saved. The detaining authorities are required to deal with such cases with more care and circumspection. They should not leave such cases to be dealt with by lower officials and should keep a track on such cases from beginning to the end and also take care that the representations, if any, made by the detenues are also dealt with expeditiously without any delay. In matters where the detention orders are passed in relation to such persons who are already in jail under some other laws, the detaining authorities should always apply their mind and show their awareness in this regard in the grounds of detention, the chances of release of such persons on bail and stating the necessity of keeping such persons in detention under the preventive detention laws. We earnestly hope that the concerned authorities shall deal with such matters with special care.[14]

15. In the result, we dismiss this special leave petition.[15]

ϸϸϸ

SEVENTEEN

HAWABI SAYED ARIF SAYED HANIF VS. L. HMINGLIANA AND ORS. (14.10.1992 – SC) : MANU/SC/0112/1993

Relative Section:

Conservation Of Foreign Exchange And Prevention Of Smuggling Activities Act, 1974 - Section 10(1), Section 3,Section 3(1), Section 3(1)(i),Section 3(1)(ii),Section 3(3), Section 8, Section 8(b), Section 8(c), Section 9, Section 9(1), Section 9(1)(a);

Constitution Of India - Article 22, Article 22(5);

Customs Act, 1962 - Section 108, Section 2, Section 2(d);

Prevention Of Illicit Traffic In Narcotic Drugs And Psychotropic Substances Act, 1988 - Section 10(1);

Territorial Waters, Continental Shelf, Exclusive Economic Zone And Other Maritime Zones Act, 1976 - Section 3, Territorial Waters, Continental Shelf, Exclusive Economic Zone And Other Maritime Zones Act, 1976 - Section 3(2), Territorial Waters, Continental Shelf, Exclusive Economic Zone And Other Maritime Zones Act, 1976 - Section 5

Hon'ble Judges/Coram: S.R. Pandian and R.M. Sahai, JJ.

EquivalentCitation:AIR1993SC810,1993(1)ALT(Cri)521,1993(1)BLJR248,

1993CriLJ172,
1992(3)Crimes635(SC),1993(42)ECC12,JT1992(6)SC162,1993(1)RCR(Criminal)531,
1992(2)SCALE796, (1993) 1 SCC163

Number of Pages in the Original Judgment: 10

Case Reference: Smt. Azra Fatima v. Union of India, MANU/SC/0500/ 1991; Sanjay Kumar Aggarwal v. Union of India, MANU/SC/0461/1990;

Case Note:

Customs - Validity of detention - Section 3 of Conservation of Foreign Exchange and Prevention of Smuggling Activities Act, 1974 - First Respondent passed order of detention against detenu with a view to preventing him from smuggling of goods - High Court dismissed Petition filed, challenging impugned detention - Hence, this Appeal - Whether, there was a clear nexus between detenu and his activities of smuggling goods within State of Maharashtra - Held, a perusal of grounds of detention clearly showed that almost all arrangements were made for disposal of smuggled silver ingots - Apprehended activities of smuggling by detenu have a territorial nexus with the State of Maharashtra - Detenu was a resident of Bombay - Therefore, detaining authority legitimately drawing his subjective satisfaction that in future also smuggling activities of detenu may take place within State of Maharashtra - Thus, detaining authority had passed detention order in exercise of his powers under Section 3(1) of Act - Hence, there was a clear nexus between detenu and his activities of smuggling goods within State of Maharashtra - Appeal dismissed.

Ratio Decidendi : "It is not law that no order of detention can validly be passed against a person in custody under any circumstances."

Facts:

1. The factual matrix of the case in a short compass can be stated as follows:[3]

In pursuance of the information collected by the officers of the Directorate of Revenue Intelligence, a surveillance was maintained by the officers on Coast Guard vessel O.G. 'VIGRAH' in the sea off Karwar for a suspect Arab Dhow carrying foreign silver to smuggle into India. During surveillance around 23.00 hours on 25.9.90, the officers sighted an Arab Dhow about 3 to 5 nautical miles away from Karwar harbour. On suspicion the officers signalled with loud speakers and search lights to stop the said Dhow, but instead of stopping, the Dhow started speeding away in the opposite direction. Seeing this, the officers fired in the air and warned the crew on the Arab Dhow to bring it alongside the ship. Thereafter the Dhow stopped and came alongside the coast guard ship and the officers from the coast' guard ship boarded the Dhow. On examination, the officers found 150 packages containing contraband silver ingots on board. There were nine persons on board. The silver ingots were seized and those nine persons were escorted by the coast guard ship to Mole Station, Ballard Pier, Bombay. The silver packages were unloaded in the presence of 2 panchas and the 9 persons were arrested. The total quantity of the contrabands was weighing 4738,901 kgs. and valued at Rs. 3,31,72,507/-. Besides the contrabands on a rummage the officers recovered 17 empty unused cloth jackets generally used for packing contraband gold with 4 documents and 11 seaman cards from the Dhow. The officers seized the silver in the reasonable belief that it was smuggled into India and hence liable for confiscation under the Customs Act, 1962. The other articles were also seized.

Held, while allowing the appeal

1. This contention relates to the non-placing of the full text of the remand order of Sayed Arif Sayed Hanif before the detaining authority. A similar contention was raised before the High Court, but it was rejected. The remand application No. 981/90 dated 28.9.90 was made in respect of the crew members. A copy of this remand application is annexed to the grounds of detention. At the foot of the remand application there is an endorsement to the effect that all the accused produced before the court were remanded in judicial custody till 11.10.1990. Though the full text of the remand order was not placed before the detaining authority, the substance of the same was placed. We are in complete agreement with the High Court that the non-placing of the remand order before the detaining authority has in no way effected either the subjective satisfaction of the authority or the detenu's right to make a detailed representation.[33]

2. Incidently, Mr. R.K. Jain advanced an argument that this is a case of abetting the smuggling of goods but not smuggling goods and, therefore, the detention order should have been made under Section 3(1)(ii) of the Act but not under Section 3(1)(i). Admittedly, this ground has not been urged either before the High Court or in the grounds of appeal or in the writ petition. When it was pointed out to the learned Counsel, he did not press this contention. However, after going through the entire documents, we see no force in this submission. The impugned order is passed under Section 3(1) of the Act in general.[34]

3. For the discussions made above we find no merit in any one of the contentions advanced questioning the legality of the impugned order of

detention. In the result, the appeal is dismissed.[35]

Writ Petition No. 76/92

For the reasons given above in the Criminal Appeal, this Writ Petition also stands dismissed.[36]

ᐅᐅᐅ

EIGHTEEN

Azra Fatima vs. Union of India (UOI) and Ors. (12.07.1990 - SC) : MANU/SC/0500/1991

Relative Section:

Constitution Of India - Article 22, Article 22(5);

Narcotic Drugs And Psychotropic Substances Act, 1985 - Section 67;

Prevention Of Illicit Traffic In Narcotic Drugs And Psychotropic Substances Act, 1988 - Section 10,Section 10(1), Section 3, Section 3(1)

Hon'ble Judges/Coram: B.C. Ray and N.M. Kasliwal, JJ.

Equivalent Citation: AIR1990SC1763, 1990 (27) ACC 573, 1990(92)BOMLR515, 1990CriLJ1731, 1991(53)ELT208(S.C.), JT1990(3)SC156, (1991)1SCC76, [1990]3SCR268

Number of Pages in the Original Judgment: 8

Case Reference:

N. Meera Rani v. Government of Tamil Nadu, MANU/SC/0381/1989; Sanjeev Kumar Aggarwal v. Union of India, MANU/SC/0461/1990; Smt. Shashi Aggarwal v. State of U.P. MANU/SC/0457/1988 ; Ramesh Yadav v. District Magistrate Etah, MANU/SC/0098/1985; Dharmendra Sugan Chand Chelwat v. Union of India and Ors. MANU/SC/0226/1990

Case Note:

Criminal - preventive detention - Sections 3 and 10 of Narcotics Drugs and Psychotropic Substances Act, 1988 - petitioner contended mere possibility of release of detenue from custody not enough for preventive detention and declaration issued under Section 10 (1) served on detenue after unexplained delay of 21 days sufficient enough for quashing of detention order - order of detention is not illegal on ground of being passed while detenue being in custody if facts and circumstances otherwise justifies order - principle of five days and fifteen days as provided in Sub-section 3 of Section 3 relating to communication of grounds of detention cannot be applied in respect of declaration issued under Section 10 (1) - held, detention order legal.

Facts:

1. Syed Ali Raza Shafiq Mohammed was detained by an order of detection passed under Section 3(1) of the Prevention of Illicit Traffic in Narcotic Drugs and Psychotropic Substances Act, 1988 (hereinafter referred to as the Act) dated 19.12.88 by the Secretary (II) to the Government of Maharashtra, Home Department. The detention order and the grounds of detention were given to the detenu on 20th December, 1988. It may be mentioned that on 19.12.99 the detenu was already in jail as his bail application had been rejected. The wife of the detenu filed a writ petition before the Bombay High Court challenging the detention of her husband Syed Ali Raza Shafiq Mohammed. The Division Bench of the High Court dismissed the writ petition by order dated 29th September, 1989. The wife of the detenu has now filed the present Special Leave Petition aggrieved against the Judgment of the Bombay High Court. Learned counsel for the petitioner raised the following submissions before us: [2]

(1) There were no prospects ,of the detenu being enlarged on bail as he was involved in a case under the Act where the offence was punishable with minimum sentence of ten years. The bail application filed on behalf of the detenu was rejected by the Metropolitan Magistrate and the detenu had not filed any application for bail either in the Sessions Court or in the High Court.

(2) That detention orders of Rai Chand Shah and Jai Lal Vora had already been struck down by the High Court on the ground that the medical report in respect of the injury sustained by Rai Chand Shah was placed in a truncated form before the detaining authority. The detention order of the present detenu also suffers from the same vice and as such his order of

detention should also be set aside.

(3) That a declaration was issued under Section 10(1) of the Act on 20th January, 1989 and the said declaration was served on the detenu after an unexplained delay of 21 days.

(4) The detenu submitted a representation on 31.1.89 which was jointly addressed to the Government of Maharashtra and the government of India and the Hon'ble Advisory Board for revocation of the impugned order of detention. The State Government rejected the representation by its reply dated 21.2.89 and the Central Government by its reply dated 3.3.89. Thus there was an inordinate and unexplained delay in considering the said representations of the detenu and this violated the right of the detenu under Article 22(5) of the Constitution of India. The order of detention , is illegal on this count also.

Held, while allowing the appeal

1. The last submission made on behalf of the detenu is that the detenu had submitted a representation on 31.1.89 jointly addressed to the Government of Maharashtra, the Government of India and the Advisory Board. The State Government rejected the representation by its reply dated 21.2.89 and the Central Government by its reply dated 3.3.89. It was thus contended that there was an inordinate and unexplained delay in considering the said representations and this is violative of the right of the detenu conferred under Clause (5) of Article 22 of the Constitution. The point should not detain us any longer as we fully agree with the finding of the High Court, recorded in this regard. The High Court has given adequate and detailed reasons in holding that the delay has been explained by the counter affidavit filed by the respondents. Thus we find no force in this ground of the detenu that his representations were disposed of after an inordinate and unexplained delay.[19]

2. As a result of the above discussion, we find no force in this petition and it is accordingly dismissed.[20]

ppp

NINETEEN

Dev Shankar Mishra and Ors. vs. Union of India and Ors. (05.05.2017 - ALLHC) : MANU/UP/1080/2017

Relative Section:

Constitution Of India - Article 226, Constitution Of India - Article 227, Constitution Of India - Article 32; Customs Act, 1962 - Section 118; Narcotic Drugs And Psychotropic Substances Act, 1985 - Section 15, Narcotic Drugs And Psychotropic Substances Act, 1985 - Section 17, Narcotic Drugs And Psychotropic Substances Act, 1985 - Section 18, Narcotic Drugs And Psychotropic Substances Act, 1985 - Section 19, Narcotic Drugs And Psychotropic Substances Act, 1985 - Section 68-A (2)(cc), Narcotic Drugs And Psychotropic Substances Act, 1985 - Section 68-A(2)(c), Narcotic Drugs And Psychotropic Substances Act, 1985 - Section 68-E, Narcotic Drugs And Psychotropic Substances Act, 1985 - Section 68-E (1), Narcotic Drugs And Psychotropic Substances Act, 1985 - Section 68-F, Narcotic Drugs And Psychotropic Substances Act, 1985 - Section 68-F (1), Narcotic Drugs And Psychotropic Substances Act, 1985 - Section 68-F (2), Narcotic Drugs And Psychotropic Substances Act, 1985 - Section 68-F(2), Narcotic Drugs And Psychotropic Substances Act, 1985 - Section 68-H (1), Narcotic Drugs And

Psychotropic Substances Act, 1985 - Section 68-I, Narcotic Drugs And Psychotropic Substances Act, 1985 - Section 68-I(1), Narcotic Drugs And Psychotropic Substances Act, 1985 - Section 68-K, Narcotic Drugs And Psychotropic Substances Act, 1985 - Section 68-L, Narcotic Drugs And Psychotropic Substances Act, 1985 - Section 68-O, Narcotic Drugs And Psychotropic Substances Act, 1985 - Section 68-U, Narcotic Drugs And Psychotropic Substances Act, 1985 - Section 68-Z, Narcotic Drugs And Psychotropic Substances Act, 1985 - Section 68A(2)(a), Narcotic Drugs And Psychotropic Substances Act, 1985 - Section 68E, Narcotic Drugs And Psychotropic Substances Act, 1985 - Section 68F, Narcotic Drugs And Psychotropic Substances Act, 1985 - Section 68H(1), Narcotic Drugs And Psychotropic Substances Act, 1985 - Section 68K, Narcotic Drugs And Psychotropic Substances Act, 1985 - Section 68L, Narcotic Drugs And Psychotropic Substances Act, 1985 - Section 8; Prevention Of Illicit Traffic In Narcotic Drugs And Psychotropic Substances Act, 1988 - Section 3(1)

Hon'ble Judges/Coram: Dr. Devendra Kumar Arora and Ravindra Nath Mishra-II, JJ.

Equivalent Citation: 2017(6)ADJ395, 2017(176)AIC872, 2017(4) ALJ 328, 2017 (100) ACC 145, 2017 3 AWC2758All

Number of Pages in the Original Judgment: 9

Case Reference:

Thansingh Nathmal and Ors. vs. A. Mazid, Superintendent of Taxes MANU/SC/0255/1964; Titaghur Paper Mills Co. Ltd. and Anr. vs. State of Orissa and Ors. MANU/SC/0317/1983; Secretary of State vs. Mask and Co. MANU/PR/0022/1940; Mafatlal Industries Ltd. and Ors. vs. Union of India (UOI) and Ors. MANU/SC/1203/1997; L. Chandra Kumar vs. Union of India and others MANU/SC/0261/1997; Karnataka Chemical Industries & Ors. vs. Union of India & Ors. MANU/SC/0439/1999; Central Coalfields Ltd. vs. State of Jharkhand and Ors. MANU/SC/0535/2005; United Bank of India vs. Satyawati Tondon and Ors. MANU/SC/0541/2010; Kanaiyalal Lalchand Sachdev and Ors. vs. State of Maharashtra and Ors. MANU/SC/0103/2011; City and Industrial Development Corporation vs. Dosu Aardeshir Bhiwandiwala and Ors. MANU/SC/8250/2008; Commissioner of Income Tax and Ors. vs. Chhabil Dass Agarwal MANU/SC/0802/2013; Whirlpool Corporation vs. Registrar of Trade Marks, Mumbai & Ors. MANU/SC/0664/1998; Aftab Abdul Rehman Chatriwala vs. State of Karnataka and others MANU/KA/0063/1994; Union of India (UOI) and Anr. vs. Vicco Laboratories MANU/SC/4450/2007

Case Note:

(1) Narcotic Drugs and Psychotropic Substances Act, 1985 - Section 68--Constitution of India--Article 226--Forfeiture of property--Writ petition--Petitioners by-passed statutory alternative remedy which was not permissible--They were required to pursue that remedy and not to Invoke extra-ordinary jurisdiction of High Court to issue prerogative writ--As writ jurisdiction is meant for doing justice between parties where it could not be done in any other forum--Petitioners were at liberty to file appeal before appellate authority and agitate all ground taken herein--Writ Petition Nos. 8391 and 7953 of 2017 being not maintainable dismissed. [2], [3], [24] and [29]

(2) Narcotic Drugs and Psychotropic Substances Act, 1985--Section 68--Constitution of India-Article 226--Show-cause notice--Requiring to indicate source of income, earnings or assets--Purpose of issuance of notice was to seek reply for proposed actions before initiation of adjudication proceedings--Show cause notice was merely answerable and questionable in writ jurisdiction--Writ Petition Nos. 4692, 5231 and 5236 of 2017 being not maintainable dismissed. [28] and [32]

Facts:

1. In the aforesaid Writ Petition No. 8391 (MB) of 2017 and 7953 (MB) of 2017, petitioners have challenged the order dated 16.03.2017 passed by the Competent Authority and Administrator, SAFEM (FOP)A & NDPSA, New Delhi under Section 68-I(1) & (3) of the Narcotics Drugs and Psychotropic Substances Act (in short "NDPS Act"), whereby the properties mentioned therein has been forfeited to the Central Government free from all encumbrances. The petitioners have also challenged the consequential order dated 17.03.2017 passed under Section 68-U of the NDPS Act, whereby the petitioners have been asked to surrender possession of the properties mentioned in the order within 30 days of the service of the order.[2]

2. It is said that the petitioner-Dev Shankar Mishra was arrested on 05.03.2003 by the Officials of Narcotics Department, Lucknow at his house situates in Village Kharsatiya, Police Station Haidargarh, District Barabanki in connection with the offences under Sections 8/15/18/19 of NDPS Act. According to the prosecution case, the petitioner was arrested from his house on the basis of secret information and after search about 1109.540 Kg. Poppy Husk kept in 47 Bags as well as about 20 Kg. opium along with about Rs. 2.89 lac cash from the house and Rs. 29,100/- from the counter of Dhaba situates in Village Kharsatiya along with about 318.650 Kg. Poppy Husk was recovered and after recovery of the alleged Poppy Husk, Opium and cash

amount, the petitioner-Dev Shankar Mishra was arrested on 05.03.2003 by the officers of Narcotics Department, Lucknow.[3]

Held, while allowing the appeal

31. The Hon'ble Supreme Court and High Courts in a large number of cases have deprecated the practice of entertaining writ petitions questioning the legality of the show cause notices stalling enquiries as proposed and retarding investigation process to find actual facts with the participation. Unless the High Court is satisfied that the show cause notice was totally honest in the eyes of law for absolute want of jurisdiction of the authority to even investigate into the fact, writ petitioners will not be entertained for the mere asking and as a matter of routine. The writ petitioners in such cases are directed to respond to the show cause notice and take all stands highlighted in the writ petition before the Adjudicating Authority.[31]

32. Issuance of show cause notice is a statutory provision subject to limitation. The purpose of its issuance is to seek a reply for the proposed actions thereunder, before initiation of adjudication proceedings. In other words, show cause notice is merely answerable and not questionable in a writ proceeding. Therefore, afore-captioned writ petitions [writ petition Nos. 4692, 5231 and 5236 of 2017 (M/B)] are not maintainable and are liable to be dismissed. Even otherwise, in view of the passing of final order dated 16.3.2017, these writ petitions are rendered infructuous and are hereby dismissed as such.[32]

ppp

TWENTY

Thana Singh vs. Central Bureau of Narcotics (30.08.2010 - SC) : MANU/SC/1303/2010

Relative Section:

Prevention of Illicit Traffic in Narcotic Drugs and Psychotropic Substances Act, 1988 - Section 8; NARCOTIC DRUGS AND PSYCHOTROPIC SUBSTANCES ACT, 1985 - Section 29, NARCOTIC DRUGS AND PSYCHOTROPIC SUBSTANCES ACT, 1985 - Section 37; Constitution of India - Article 21

Hon'ble Judges/Coram: Devinder Kumar Jain and H.L. Dattu, JJ.

Equivalent Citation: 2013(3) RCR (Criminal) 931, (2013) 2SCC603

Number of Pages in the Original Judgment: 2

Case Reference:

Prisoners v. Union of India and Ors.1994 (3) R.C.R. (Criminal) 639 : MANU/SC/0877/1994:1994 (6) SCC 731

Case Note:

Trial for an offence under Section 8 read with Section 29 of the Narcotic Drugs and Psychotropic Substances Act, 1988 (for short, "the NDPS Act")- Accused is languishing in jail for a period of over twelve years and yet the conclusion of the trial is not in sight. Aggrieved by the order passed by the High Court of Madhya Pradesh in Misc. Criminal Case No. 6036 of 2009 whereby appellant's application for grant of bail has been dismissed.

Facts:

Leave granted. This is yet another unfortunate case where an accused, facing trial for an offence under Section 8 read with Section 29 of the Narcotic Drugs and Psychotropic Substances Act, 1988 (for short, "the NDPS Act"), is languishing in jail for a period of over twelve years and yet the conclusion of the trial is not in sight. Admittedly, the appellant has been in judicial custody since 13th April, 1998. Aggrieved by the order passed by the High Court of Madhya Pradesh in Misc. Criminal Case No. 6036 of 2009 whereby appellant's application for grant of bail has been dismissed, he has knocked at the door of this Court for appropriate relief. Vide order dated 16th August, 2010, we had directed the Assistant Commissioner (Narcotics) Neemuch to file an affidavit explaining the cause for undue delay in trial. Simultaneously, we had also requested the Special Judge, NDPS, Mandsaur (M.P.) to send a report regarding the present status of the trial. In response thereto, the Deputy Narcotics Commissioner, Neemuch (M.P.) has filed an affidavit wherein it is stated that there is no delay on the part of the said Bureau and "it appears from the record that the delay has been occasioned either due to appellant or other co-accused persons." As regards the present stage of trial, it is pointed out that 16 witnesses have already been examined by the prosecution and there is every possibility of the trial being concluded within a short period.

Held, while allowing the appeal

1. Time and again, this Court has emphasized the need for speedy trial, particularly when the release of an undertrial on bail is restricted under the provisions of the statute, like in the present case under Section 37 of the NDPS Act. While considering the question of grant of bail to an accused facing trial under the NDPS Act in Supreme Court Legal Aid Committee representing undertrial Prisoners v. Union of India and Ors. MANU/SC/0877/1994 : 1994 (3) R.C.R. (Criminal) 639 : 1994 (6) SCC 731 , this Court had observed that though some amount of deprivation of personal liberty cannot be avoided in such cases, but if the period of deprivation, pending trial, becomes unduly long, the fairness assured by Article 21 of the Constitution would receive a jolt. It was further observed that after the accused person has suffered imprisonment, which is half

of the maximum punishment provided for the offence, any further deprivation of personal liberty would be violative of the fundamental right visualized by Article 21. We regret to note that despite it all, there has not been visible improvement on this front.[3]

1. Bearing in mind these observations and having regard to the fact that in the present case the appellant has been in custody for more than 12 years and seemingly there being no prospect of the conclusion of trial in the near future, we are of the opinion that it is a fit case where he deserves to be admitted to bail forthwith.[4]

3. Accordingly, the appeal is allowed; the impugned order is set aside and it is directed that the appellant shall be granted bail till the conclusion of the trial, subject to the following conditions:[5]

i) The appellant shall furnish personal bond in the sum of ` 20,000/- with one surety in the like amount to the satisfaction of the trial Court;

(ii) the appellant shall report to the trial Court on every 1st and 14th of the Calendar month at 10.00 a.m.;

(iii) the appellant shall not leave the jurisdictional area of the trial court without the permission of the Court.

(iv) If any of these conditions are violated, or a case for cancellation of bail is made out, the trial court will be at liberty to cancel the bail.

4. We would also direct the trial Court to expedite the trial and try to conclude it within one year from the date of receipt of a copy of this order. Before parting with the case, we also deem it necessary to issue notice to all the States through their Chief Secretaries to furnish information of all the cases where the under trials in cases under the NDPS Act have been in incarceration for a period of five years or more. The office shall take appropriate steps to send a copy of this order to all the States for compliance. Requisite affidavits shall be filed within eight weeks. List immediately after eight weeks for further directions.[6]

ᏜᏜᏜ

TWENTY-ONE

NKGSB Cooperative Bank Limited vs. Subir Chakravarty and Ors. (25.02.2022 - SC) : MANU/SC/0247/2022

Relative Section:

Andhra Pradesh Reorganisation Act, 2014 - Section 86; Arms Act 1959 - Section 24A, Arms Act 1959 - Section 24B, Arms Act 1959 - Section 43; Army Act, 1950 - Section 47; Banning Of Unregulated Deposit Schemes Act, 2019 - Section 31; Bihar Reorganisation Act, 2000 - Section 80; Central Goods And Services Tax Act, 2017 - Section 107, Central Goods And Services Tax Act, 2017 - Section 108, Central Goods And Services Tax Act, 2017 - Section 112, Central Goods And Services Tax Act, 2017 - Section 5; Central Reserve Police Force Act 1949 - Section 2(g); Chemical Weapons Convention Act, 2000 - Section 22, Chemical Weapons Convention Act, 2000 - Section 23, Chemical Weapons Convention Act, 2000 - Section 24, Chemical Weapons Convention Act, 2000 - Section 37; Child And Adolescent Labour (prohibition And Regulation) Act, 1986 - Section 17A; Children Act, 1960 - Section 56; Code of Civil Procedure, 1908 (CPC) - Order XXVI Rule 17; Code of Criminal

Procedure, 1973 (CrPC) - Section 12; Code of Criminal Procedure, 1973 (CrPC) - Section 154; Code of Criminal Procedure, 1973 (CrPC) - Section 165; Code of Criminal Procedure, 1973 (CrPC) - Section 17; Code of Criminal Procedure, 1973 (CrPC) - Section 284; Code of Criminal Procedure, 1973 (CrPC) - Section 34; Code of Criminal Procedure, 1973 (CrPC) - Section 55; Conservation Of Foreign Exchange And Prevention Of Smuggling Activities Act, 1974 - Section 12; Constitution Of India - Article 154, Constitution Of India - Article 226, Constitution Of India - Article 227, Constitution Of India - Article 311, Constitution Of India - Article 311(1), Constitution Of India - Article 53; Customs Act, 1962 - Section 129D, Customs Act, 1962 - Section 129DA, Customs Act, 1962 - Section 28J, Customs Act, 1962 - Section 5; Delhi Police Act, 1978 - Section 12, Delhi Police Act, 1978 - Section 122, Delhi Police Act, 1978 - Section 147, Delhi Police Act, 1978 - Section 20, Delhi Police Act, 1978 - Section 21, Delhi Police Act, 1978 - Section 25, Delhi Police Act, 1978 - Section 3, Delhi Police Act, 1978 - Section 58, Delhi Police Act, 1978 - Section 64, Delhi Police Act, 1978 - Section 70; Delhi Rent Act, 1995 - Section 44; Employee's Compensation Act, 1923 - Section 2(1), Employee's Compensation Act, 1923 - Section 2(f); Export (quality Control And Inspection) Act, 1963 - Section 10K, Export (quality Control And Inspection) Act, 1963 - Section 10M, Export (quality Control And Inspection) Act, 1963 - Section 13; Food Safety And Standards Act, 2006 - Section 30; Foreign Trade (development And Regulation) Act, 1992 - Section 11, Foreign Trade (development And Regulation) Act, 1992 - Section 15, Foreign Trade (development And Regulation) Act, 1992 - Section 16, Foreign Trade (development And Regulation) Act, 1992 - Section 6; Fugitive Economic Offenders Act, 2018 - Section 8; General Clauses Act 1897 - Section 3(5); Guardians And Wards Act, 1890 - Section 4A; Hotel-receipts Tax Act, 1980 - Section 23; Human Immunodeficiency Virus And Acquired Immune Deficiency Syndrome (prevention And Control) Act, 2017 - Section 45; Indian Coconut Committee Act, 1944 - Section 2(a); Indian Evidence Act, 1872 - Section 121; Indian Penal Code 1860, (IPC) - Section 165; Indian Penal Code 1860, (IPC) - Section 376; Indian Succession Act, 1925 - Section 195; Industrial Disputes Act, 1947 - Section 39; Industrial Employment (standing Orders) Act, 1946 - Section 14A; Industrial Relations Code, 2020 - Section 100; Insurance Act, 1938 - Section 110A, Insurance Act, 1938 - Section 110B, Insurance Act, 1938 - Section 34H; Legal Metrology Act, 2009 - Section 54; Mahatma Gandhi National Rural Employment Guarantee Act, 2005 - Section 26; Maintenance And Welfare Of Parents And Senior Citizens Act 2007 - Section 22; Manipur Land Revenue

And Land Reforms Act, 1960 - Section 166, Manipur Land Revenue And Land Reforms Act, 1960 - Section 5, Manipur Land Revenue And Land Reforms Act, 1960 - Section 68, Manipur Land Revenue And Land Reforms Act, 1960 - Section 7, Manipur Land Revenue And Land Reforms Act, 1960 - Section 84, Manipur Land Revenue And Land Reforms Act, 1960 - Section 93, Manipur Land Revenue And Land Reforms Act, 1960 - Section 95, Manipur Land Revenue And Land Reforms Act, 1960 - Section 96; Narcotic Drugs And Psychotropic Substances Act, 1985 - Section 41; National Security Act, 1980 - Section 14; New Delhi Municipal Council Act, 1994 - Section 328, New Delhi Municipal Council Act, 1994 - Section 46; Orphanages And Other Charitable Homes (supervision And Control) Act, 1960 - Section 5; Passports Act, 1967 - Section 21; Police Act, 1861 - Section 2, Police Act, 1861 - Section 7; Prevention Of Illicit Traffic In Narcotic Drugs And Psychotropic Substances Act, 1988 - Section 13; Prevention Of Money-laundering Act, 2002 - Section 17; Prisons Act, 1894 - Section 22, Prisons Act, 1894 - Section 48, Prisons Act, 1894 - Section 8; Punjab Reorganisation Act, 1966 - Section 79; Railways Act, 1989 - Section 93; Requisitioning And Acquisition Of Immovable Property Act, 1952 - Section 17, Requisitioning And Acquisition Of Immovable Property Act, 1952 - Section 23; Right To Fair Compensation And Transparency In Land Acquisition, Rehabilitation And Resettlement Act, 2013 - Section 43; Securitisation And Reconstruction Of Financial Assets And Enforcement Of Security Interest Act, 2002 - Section 13, Securitisation And Reconstruction Of Financial Assets And Enforcement Of Security Interest Act, 2002 - Section 13(2), Securitisation And Reconstruction Of Financial Assets And Enforcement Of Security Interest Act, 2002 - Section 13(4), Securitisation And Reconstruction Of Financial Assets And Enforcement Of Security Interest Act, 2002 - Section 14, Securitisation And Reconstruction Of Financial Assets And Enforcement Of Security Interest Act, 2002 - Section 14(1), Securitisation And Reconstruction Of Financial Assets And Enforcement Of Security Interest Act, 2002 - Section 14(1-A), Securitisation And Reconstruction Of Financial Assets And Enforcement Of Security Interest Act, 2002 - Section 14(1A), Securitisation And Reconstruction Of Financial Assets And Enforcement Of Security Interest Act, 2002 - Section 14(2), Securitisation And Reconstruction Of Financial Assets And Enforcement Of Security Interest Act, 2002 - Section 14(3), Securitisation And Reconstruction Of Financial Assets And Enforcement Of Security Interest Act, 2002 - Section 38, Securitisation And Reconstruction Of Financial Assets And Enforcement Of Security Interest Act, 2002 - Section

6(b); Security Interest (enforcement) Rules, 2002 - Rule 2(a), Security Interest (enforcement) Rules, 2002 - Rule 8, Security Interest (enforcement) Rules, 2002 - Rule 8(3), Security Interest (enforcement) Rules, 2002 - Rule 9; Suppression Of Immoral Traffic In Women And Girls Act, 1956 - Section 14; Unlawful Activities (prevention) Act, 1967 - Section 42, Unlawful Activities (prevention) Act, 1967 - Section 43A; Uttar Pradesh Consolidation Of Holdings Act, 1953 - Section 48; Uttar Pradesh Reorganisation Act, 2000 - Section 81; Wild Life (protection) Act, 1972 - Section 5

Hon'ble Judges/Coram:

A.M. Khanwilkar and C.T. Ravikumar, JJ.

Equivalent Citation: 2022(3)ABR182, 2022(233)AIC220, AIR2022SC1325, 2022(2)ALLMR854, I(2022)BC612(SC), 2022(2)BomCR410, 2022 (1) CCC 381 , 2022GLH(2)1, 2022/INSC/238, 2022(2)RCR(Civil)414, (2022)10SCC286, 2022 (2) SCJ 319, [2022]171SCL310(SC), [2022]1SCR1177

Number of Pages in the Original Judgment: 25

Case Reference:

Muhammed Ashraf and Ors. v. Union of India (UOI) MANU/KE/0456/2008; Federal Bank Limited v. A.V. Punnus MANU/KE/1086/2013; Sakiri Vasu v. State of U.P. and Ors. MANU/SC/8179/2007; Dattatreya Moreshwar Pangarkar v. The State of Bombay and Ors. MANU/SC/0014/1952; Sangram Singh v. Election Tribunal, Kotah and Ors. MANU/SC/0044/1955; A.S.T. Arunachalam Pillai v. Southern Roadways (Private) Ltd. MANU/SC/0249/1960; S. Krishnaswamy Mudaliar and Ors. v. P.S. Palani Pillai and Ors. MANU/TN/0237/1957; B. Veeraswamy and Ors. v. State of Andhra Pradesh represented by its Secretary, Public Works and Transport Department, Hyderabad and Ors. MANU/AP/0192/1959; R.G. Jacob v. Union of India (UOI) MANU/SC/0140/1962; Government of A.P. and Ors. v. N. Ramanaiah MANU/SC/0815/2009; Raghunath Sahai v. Sarup Singh MANU/UP/0147/1962; Ram Narain and Ors. v. Director of Consolidation and Ors. MANU/UP/0050/1965; Laxminarayan Sarangi v. State of Orissa and Ors. MANU/OR/0002/1963; Mahadev Prasad Roy v. S.N. Chatterjee and Ors. MANU/BH/0097/1954; Gurmukh Singh v. Union of India (UOI), New Delhi MANU/PH/0102/1963; Rao Shiv Bahadur Singh and Ors. v. The State of Vindhya Pradesh MANU/SC/0081/1953; Lalit Mohan Das v. Advocate-General, Orissa MANU/SC/0019/1956; O.P. Sharma and Ors. v. High Court of Punjab and Haryana MANU/SC/0571/2011; Satheedevi v. Prasanna and Ors. MANU/SC/0367/2010; Hiralal Rattanlal and Ors. v. State of U.P. and Ors. MANU/SC/0553/1972; Dipak Babaria and Ors. v. State of Gujarat and Ors. MANU/SC/0052/2014; V.S.

Sunitha v. Federal Bank Ltd.; S. Chandramohan and Anr. v. The Chief Metropolitan Magistrate, Egmore, Chennai and Ors. MANU/TN/2503/2014 : 2014-5-L.W. 620; Rahul Chaudhary v. Andhra Bank and Ors.; J. Marks Exim (India) Pvt. Ltd. v. Punjab National Bank; Mahadev Govind Gharge and Ors. v. Special Land Acquisition Officer, Upper Krishna Project, Jamkhandi, Karnataka MANU/SC/0597/2011 : (2011) 6 SCC 321; Federal Deposit Ins. Corporation v. Winton, C.C.A. Tenn. MANU/FEST/0054/1942 : 131 F.2d 780; Slegel v. Slegel 135 N.J. Eq. 5 : 37 A.2d 57; Doherty v. King, Tex. Civ. App. 183 S.W.2d 1004; Donohue v. Zoning Bd. of Appeals of Town of Norwalk 155 Conn. 550 : 235 A.2d 643; Authorised Officer, Indian Bank v. D. Visalakshi and Anr. MANU/SC/1303/2019 : (2019) 20 SCC 47

Case Note:

Banking - Possession of Secured Assets and documents - Appointment of Advocate for such purpose - Section 14(1A) of the Securitisation and Reconstruction of Financial Assets and Enforcement of Security Interest Act, 2002 - Whether District Magistrate or the Chief Metropolitan Magistrate can appoint an advocate and authorise him/her to take possession as provided for in the statute?

Facts:

The Bombay High Court vide its relevant judgment opined that the advocate, not being a subordinate officer to the CMM or DM, such appointment would be illegal. Against this decision, four separate appeals were filed by the concerned parties. On the other hand, the High Court of Madras took a contrary view that the advocate is regarded as an officer of the court and, thus, subordinate to the CMM or the DM. Against this decision, a special leave petition was filed by the borrowers. The High Courts of Kerala and Delhi have taken the same view. Hence the present appeals to adjudicate on whether Advocate can be appointment as one authorised to take possession of secured assets and connected document.

Held, while disposing the Appeals:

It is well established that an advocate is a guardian of constitutional morality and justice equally with the Judge. He has an important duty as that of a Judge. He bears responsibility towards the society and is expected to act with utmost sincerity and commitment to the cause of justice. He has a duty to the court first. As an officer of the court, he owes allegiance to a higher cause and cannot indulge in consciously misstating the facts or for that matter conceal any material fact within his knowledge.[39]

There is no reason to assume that the advocate so appointed by the CMM/DM would misuse the task entrusted to him/her and that will not be carried out strictly as per law or it would be a case of abuse of power. Rather, going by the institutional faith or trust reposed on advocates being officers of the court, there must be a presumption that if an advocate is appointed as commissioner for execution of the orders passed by the CMM/DM under Section 14(1) of the 2002 Act, that responsibility and duty will be discharged honestly and in accordance with Rules of law.[42]

A fortiori, the judgment and order of the Bombay High Court impugned in the present appealsis declared as not a good law. Whereas, the conclusion of the three High Courts, namely, High Courts of Kerala, Madras and Delhi on the question under consideration upheld.[45]

Theappeals filed by the secured creditors are allowed. Resultantly, the impugned judgment and order passed by the Bombay High Court is set aside and the subject writ petition stands dismissed.The special leave petition filed by the borrowers against the impugned judgment and order of the Madras High Court is delinked for being heard for admission, on the limited issue regarding compliance or non-compliance of Clauses (i) to (ix) of Section 14 of the 2002 Act in the fact situation of the present case.[47]

Industry: Banks

ppp

Adv. Jayprakash Somani's Videos On Law

Adv. Jayprakash Somani's Videos on Law on Youtube- 'jaysomani64' channel.

1) SLP in Supreme Court / Special Leave Petitions in the Supreme Court of India

2) Transfer of Civil & Criminal Cases by the Supreme Court of India / Transfer of Matrimonial Cases

3) Appellate Jurisdiction of the Supreme Court of India

4) Jurisdictions of the Supreme Court of India

5) Public Interest Litigation in the Supreme Court of India / PIL in Supreme Court

6) Article 32 Writ Petitions in the Supreme Court of India

7) Bail Matters Top 10 Supreme Court Cases

8) FIR Quashing in High Court & Supreme Court

9) Bail & Anticipatory Bail Matters in Supreme Court

10) Insolvency & Bankruptcy Matters in the Supreme Court

11) Insolvency & Bankruptcy Code 2016 Part 1

12) Insolvency & Bankruptcy Code 2016 Part 2

13) Insolvency & Bankruptcy Code 2016 Part 3

14) Corporate Liquidation Process

15) Supreme Court Rules & Procedures Webinar of 2.5 hour on Zoom

16) RDDBFI Act, 1993 (Introduction)

17) The Indian Contact Act 1872

18) Negotiable Instruments Act (Introduction)

19) How to avoid matrimonial disputes& some more videos

20) SEBI Matters in the Supreme Court

21) Matrimonial Matters: Supreme Court's 20 Case Laws

22) Consumer Matters Supreme Court's 20 Case Laws

23) Service Matters Supreme Court's 20 Case Laws

24) How to Search Lawyer for Your Matter

25) Property Matters Supreme Court's 20 Case Laws

26) Bail Matters: Supreme Court's 20 Case Laws

27) Supreme Court / High Court Vacation Benches

28) 69000 Teacher's Recruitment Matters of UP Government in the Supreme Court

29) Contempt of Court Matters in the Supreme Court

30) Advocate Act's Matters in the Supreme Court

31) Business Law Matters in the Supreme Court

32) Banking Matters in the Supreme Court

33) Labour Law Matters in the Supreme Court

34) Arbitration Matters in the Supreme Court

35) Careers in Law -Zoom Webinar by Adv. Jayprakash Somani

36) Civil Matters in the Supreme Court

37) Consumer Protection Act | Consumer Matters in the Supreme Court

38) Corporate Matters in the Supreme Court

39) Criminal Matters in the Supreme Court

40) Role of Respondent in the Supreme Court of India

41) Motor Vehicle Accident Matters in Supreme Court with case laws

42) Article 131 Original Suits in Supreme Court

43) PIL in Supreme Court/ Public Interest Litigations in the Supreme Court of India'

44) CAB Citizenship Amendment Bill is not Unconstitutional

45) Supreme Court of India Cases & Process – Marathi

46) Legal Services Export / Export of Legal Services

47) Transfer of Matrimonial Cases by the Supreme Court of India

48) Public Interest Litigation PIL

49) The Specific Relief Act (Introduction)

50) Corporate Insolvency Resolution Process CIRP

51) ABMM's Career 5 - Careers in Law

52) Transfer of cases by Supreme Court

53) Writ Petitions in High Court & Supreme Court of India

54) Supreme Court Jurisdictions - Appeals, SLP, Writ Petitions, Transfer, Original, Review, Curative

55) LEGAL INDIA TV Show: Cases Handled in Supreme Court

56) Corporate Liquidation Process

57) Legal Services Export / Export of Legal Services

58) Corporate Laws

59) Election Matters- Supreme Court's 20 Case Laws

60) Companies Act, 2013

62) Competition Act, 2002

63) Banking Matters - Supreme Court's 20 Case Laws

64) Election Matters in the Supreme Court

65) Armed Forces Tribunal Matters in the Supreme Court

66) Compassionate Appointment Service matter

67) Foreign Exchange Management Act FEMA

68) Foreign Trade Policy 2021-26 Proposed

69) Customs Act 1962

70) Narcotic Drugs and Psychotropic Substances Act, 1985 NDPS Act

71) Foreign Trade Development & Regulation Act, 1992

72) How to Search Good Advocate in the Supreme Court of India

73) Sr. Adv Vikas Singh's Interview in Nani Palkhivala Wednesday Law Club

74) Indian Penal Code (I. P. C.)

75) Criminal Procedure Code (Cr. P. C.)

76) Commercial Courts & International Arbitration - by Mr. Jaideep Gupta, Senior Advocate in Nani Palkhivala Wednesday Law Club

77) Sr. Adv Ranji Thomos in Nani Palkhivala Wednesday Law Club

78) Urgent Matters in Supreme Court during vacations

79)498A Bail Matters in Supreme Court

81)376 Bail Matters in Supreme Court

82)302, 304, 307, 308 Bail Matters in Supreme Court

83)138, 420 Bail Matters in Supreme Court

84)POCSO Act Bail Matters in Supreme Court

85)NDPS Act Bail Matters in Supreme Court

86) What is ED (Enforcement Directorate)?

87) Prevention of Money Laundering Act, 2002 (PMLA Act)

88) Insolvency & Bankruptcy Code- Supreme Court Case Laws. Webinar in Nani Palkhivala Wednesday Law Club

89) What is NCLT & NCLAT?

90) Acquittal from 376- Supreme Court's some case laws in Nani Palkhivala Wednesday Law Club dt 28.7.22

91) Insolvency & Bankruptcy in India

92) Can we file case directly in the Supreme Court?

93) Adv. Anuja Pethia has cleared AOR Exam 2021 with 77% marks - Her interview in Nani Palkhivala Wednesday Law Club

94) Customs Act - Supreme Court Case Laws & Interview of AOR Adv. Anuja Pethia in Nani Palkhivala Law Club.

95) The Uttar Pradesh Public Service Tribunals Act, 1976

96)POCSO Act - Supreme Court Case Laws & Interview of AOR Adv. Shoumendu Mukharji & Adv. Nishant Verma in Nani Palkhivala Law Club.

97) Who Can Trigger CIRP Process Under Insolvency Law of India

98) The Uttar Pradesh Government Servant Discipline and Appeal Rules, 1999

99)CIRP Application Under Sec 7 by FC

100) Information Technology Act 2000

101) Uttar Pradesh Recruitment of Dependants of Government Servants Dying in Harness Rules, 1974

102) Foreign Exchange Management Act 1999 & Supreme Court's Case Laws on FEMA & Leading Case of AOR Exam in Nani Palkhivala Law Club.

103) Arbitration and Conciliation Act 1996 & It's Supreme Court Case Laws in Nani Palkhivala Wednesday Law Club.

104) Narcotic Drugs & Psychotropic Substances Act 1985 (NDPS Act) & It's Supreme Court Case Laws in Nani Palkhivala Wednesday Law Club.

105) Recovery of Debts and Bankruptcy Act 1993

106) Uttar Pradesh Land Revenue Code 2006

107)CIRP Application Under Sec 9 by OC

108)CIRP Application Under Sec 10 by CD

109) Hindu Succession Act, 1956

110) Maharashtra Civil Services Rules, 1981

111) Indian Contract Act, 1872 & Supreme Court's Case Laws" in Nani Palkhiwala Wednesday Law Club

112) Securities and Exchange Board of India Act, 1992 i. e. SEBI Act 1992 & Case Laws on Insiders Trading" in Nani Palkhiwala Wednesday Law Club

113) Moratorium Under Section 14 of IBC, 2016

114) Hindu Marriage Act, 1955

115) Maharashtra Land Revenue Code, 1966

116)64 Leading Cases of AOR Exam Session 1 :- Cases 1 to16 in Nani Palkhiwala Wednesday Law Club

117)64 Leading Cases of AOR Exam Session 2: Cases 17 to 32 in Nani Palkhiwala Wednesday Law Club

118)64 Leading Cases of AOR Examination Session 3: Cases 33 to 48 in Nani Palkhiwala Wednesday Law Club

119)64 Leading Cases of AOR Exam Session 4: Cases 49 to 64 in Nani Palkhiwala Wednesday Law Club

120) Labour Laws of India: Part 1 - 4 New Labour Law Codes of India

121) New Labour Laws Part 2 The Code on Wages, 2019

122) New Labour Laws Part 3:- The Code on Social Security, 2020

123) Argue in English Fluently & Confidently - Two months online course.

124) SLP Admission in the Supreme Court. 2023 (Hindi)

125) Transfer of Petitions from the Supreme Court (Hindi)

126) Review Petition in the Supreme Court.(Hindi)

127) Recovery of debts from the Company (Hindi)

128) How to search 'Good Insolvency & Bankruptcy Consultant?' (HINDI)

129) Curative Petition in the Supreme Court

130) AFT Appeals in the Supreme Court (HINDI)

131) NCLAT's Appeals in the Supreme Court.

132) Transfer Petition: Which matters can we transfer?

133) SLP Types of SLP in the Supreme court of India (English).

134) Argue in English Fluently and Confidently in the High Court & Supreme Court'.

ﺏﺏﺏ

List Of Adv. Jayprakash Somani's Published Books

1. Supreme Court of India's Leading Case Laws on 'Insolvency & Bankruptcy Code 2016'
2. Bail Matters – Supreme Court's Latest Leading Case Laws
3. Arbitration Matters- Supreme Court's Latest Leading Case Laws
4. Property Matters - Supreme Court's Latest Leading Case Laws
5. Matrimonial Matters- Supreme Court's Latest Leading Case Laws
6. Election Matters- Supreme Court's Latest Leading Case Laws
7. SEBI Matters- Supreme Court's Latest Leading Case Laws
8. Banking Matters- Supreme Court's Latest Leading Case Laws
9. Service Matters- Supreme Court's Latest Leading Case Laws
10. Contempt of Court Matters- Supreme Court's Latest Leading Case Laws
11. Consumer Protection Matters- Supreme Court's Latest Leading Case Laws
12. Corporate Law- Supreme Court's Latest Leading Case Laws
13. Supreme Court's AOR Exam- Leading Cases
14. Armed Force Tribunal - Supreme Court's Latest Leading Case Laws
15. Acquittal From 376 - Supreme Court's Latest Leading Case Laws
16. Negotiable instrument – Supreme Court's Latest Leading Case Laws
17. Contract Act- Supreme Court's Latest Leading Case Laws
18. Insider trading- Supreme Court's Latest Leading Case Laws
19. Foreign Exchange and Management Act- Supreme Court's Latest Leading Case Laws
20. Income Tax Act- Supreme Court's Latest Leading Case Laws
21. Company Law- Supreme Court's Latest Leading Case Laws
22. Competition & Monopoly Matters- Supreme Court's Latest Leading Case Laws
23. Compassionate Appointment- Service Matters- Supreme Court's Latest Leading Case Laws
24. Compulsory Retirement- Service Matters- Supreme Court's Latest Leading Case Laws
25. Voluntary Retirement- Service Matters- Supreme Court's Latest Leading Case Laws
26. Removal/Dismissal/Termination from Service- Supreme Court's Latest Leading Case Laws

27. Seniority- Service Matter- Supreme Court's Latest Leading Case Laws
28. Promotion- Service Matter- Supreme Court's Latest Leading Case Laws
29. Equal Pay for Equal Work- Service Matter- Supreme Court's Latest Leading Case Laws
30. Condition of Service- Service Matter- Supreme Court's Latest Leading Case Laws
31. Customs Act- Supreme Court's Leading Case Laws
32. Information Technology Act- Supreme Court's Leading Case Laws
33. SEC. 125 CR. P. C.- Supreme Court's Leading Case Laws
34. SEC. 498A OF I. P. C.- Supreme Court's Leading Case Laws
35. MOTOR VEHICLE ACT- Supreme Court's Leading Case Laws
36. CONDITION OF SERVICE- SERVICE MATTER- Supreme Court's Leading Case Laws
37. SUSPENSION- SERVICE MATTER- Supreme Court's Leading Case Laws
38. Reservation in SC, ST, OBC- Service Matter- Supreme Court's Leading Case Laws
39. NARCOTIC DRUGS AND PSYCHOTROPIC SUBSTANCES (NDPS) ACT - Supreme Court of India's Latest Leading Case Laws
40. SEC 302 IPC - Supreme Court of India's Latest Leading Case Laws
41. PROTECTION OF CHILDREN FROM SEXUAL OFFENCES ACT (POCSO) - Supreme Court of India's Latest Leading Case Laws
42. PMLA ACT BAIL MATTERS - Supreme Court of India's Leading Case Laws
43. SEC 376 BAIL MATTERS - Supreme Court of India's Leading Case Laws
44. SEC 302 BAIL MATTERS - Supreme Court of India's Leading Case Laws
45. POCSO ACT BAIL MATTERS - Supreme Court of India's Leading Case Laws
46. JUVENILE JUSTICE ACT- Supreme Court of India's Leading Case Laws
47. TRANSFER OF PROPERTY ACT- Supreme Court of India's Leading Case Laws
48. PROFESSIONAL ETHICS OF ADVOCATES- AOR EXAM- SUPREME COURT'S LEADING CASE LAWS
49. WHITE COLLAR CRIME- SUPREME COURT'S LEADING CASE LAWS
50. SEC 302 BAIL MATTERS- SUPREME COURT'S LEADING CASE LAWS
51. SEC 7 IBC 2016 - SUPREME COURT'S LATEST LEADING CASE LAW
52. ADVERSE POSSESSION IN PROPERTY MATTER - SUPREME COURT'S LATEST LEADING CASE LAWS
53. FOOD SAFETY AND STANDARD ACT 2006' - SUPREME COURT AND HIGH COURT's LEADING CASE LAWS

54. ARMED FORCE TRIBUNAL ACT- SUPREME COURT'S LATEST LEADING CASE LAWS

55. ESSENTIAL COMMODITIES ACT 1955- SUPREME COURT'S LATEST LEADING CASE LAWS

56. FOREIGN TRADE DEVELOPMENT AND REGULATION ACT'- SUPREME COURT AND HIGH COURT'S LEADING CASE LAWS

57. PARTNERSHIP ACT 1932- SUPREME COURT'S LEADING CASE LAWS

58. COTPA ACT 2003 - SUPREME COURT AND HIGH COURT'S LEADING CASE LAWS

59. DOMESTIC VIOLENCE ACT 2005 - SUPREME COURT'S LEADING CASE LAWS

60. DOWRY PROHIBITION ACT 1961 - SUPREME COURT'S LATEST CASE LAWS

61. SUPREME COURT'S AOR EXAM- DRAFTING Formates of more than 25 Drafts for AOR Exam Paper 2 - Drafting

62. SPECIFIC RELIEF ACT 1963- SUPREME COURT'S LATEST LEADING CASE LAWS

63. PREVENTION OF MONEY LAUNDERING ACT 2002- SUPREME COURT'S LATEST CASE LAWS

64. PREVENTION OF CORRUPTION ACT 1988- SUPREME COURT'S LATEST CASE LAWS

Books are available online in India

1. Notion Press: https://notionpress.com/author/jayprakash_somani

2. Amazon: https://www.amazon.in/s?k=jayprakash+somani

3. Flipkart: https://www.flipkart.com/search?q=Jayprakash%20Somani

Books are available online at International Market

4. Amazon International: https://www.amazon.com/s?k=jayprakash+somani

5. Amazon United Kingdom: https://www.amazon.co.uk/s?k=jayprakash+somani

6. E-Books/Kindle edition at National & International Level: https://www.amazon.in/s?k=jaypraksh+somani

❧❧❧

Adv Jayprakash Somani's Online Legal & Import Export Courses

Download our app to get access to our Free Videos, Free Bare Acts, Free Study Material in Legal as well as International Business Regime.

Android App Link ;-https://clpandrea.page.link/cmSm

Ios APp Link :-https://apps.apple.com/us/app/classplus/id1324522260

Login with org code ;- (qywzji)

Web Link ;-https://qywzji.courses.store/

Download App on Google play store - Type

<u>Jayprakash Somani SupremeCourt</u>

Legal Courses :

1. **SLP- Bail Matters- Drafting & Successful Arguing in the Supreme Court.**
2. **SLP- Succession Matters- Drafting & Successful Arguing in the Supreme Court.**
3. **Legal Vocabulary & its practice pattern to Argue in High Court and**

Supreme Court / Improve Your Legal English.
4. **SLP- Property Matters - Drafting and Successful Arguing in the Supreme Court.**

International Business Courses -

1. **Agri Products Exports - Scope from India.**
2. **Textile Exports - Scope from India.**
3. **Export Import Procedure -Perfect Documentation & It's Management.**
4. **Jewellery Exports -Scope from India.**
5. **Export Import Finance Management with LC, ECGC & Venture Capital.**
6. **Shipping & Logistics in International Business with live links of Ports, ICDs, CHAs etc.**
7. **International Business Marketing Part 1: Finding Potential & Genuine Buyers for Exports and Suppliers for Imports.**
8. **International Business Marketing Part 2: Communication Skill to take repeated orders from Potential Buyers.**

ppp